Praise for
The Ultimate Guide to Healthy Juicing

T0088219

"Michelle's book is a must-have for anyone who truly wants to fuel their body on a core level!"

—Melissa Kubek, owner of Organic Cold-Pressed Juice & Plant-Based Eats

"I've been learning from Michelle for years! She makes juicing easy, fun and delicious! Plus, her detox is perfectly outlined to make sure you succeed. In just 7 days, I lost 4 pounds and over 6 inches total!"

—Janica Larson, founder of *Simply Living With Janica*

"Michelle's book is exactly what I have been looking for since I started juicing! The recipes are delicious and easy to follow! As a yoga therapist and myofascial release practitioner, I am always looking for great information I can give my clients to keep them tuned in to their healthy transformation!"

—Yvonne Bannister, YogaMFR Therapy

"I am blown away by the recipes in this book. She is a top coach, a mom on a mission, and she is here to change the world."

—Rachel Feldman, business coach, teacher, speaker, and health coach

"Beautiful book full of delicious recipes and great advice! I haven't juiced in years, but Michelle has inspired me. A must-have book for anyone interested in optimal health and well-being!"

—Rebecca Gould, heartbreak alchemist and
award-winning author of *The Multi-Orgasmic Diet*

THE ULTIMATE GUIDE TO
HEALTHY JUICING

Also by Michelle Savage

The Green Aisle's Smoothies & Slushies
The Green Aisle's Healthy Indulgence

THE ULTIMATE GUIDE TO
HEALTHY JUICING

HOW TO USE 7-DAY AND 30-DAY JUICE CLEANSES TO BUILD STRENGTH AND LOSE WEIGHT

Michelle Savage

Skyhorse Publishing

Visit our website at www.skyhorsepublishing.com.

10 9 8 7 6 5 4 3 2

Library of Congress Cataloging-in-Publication Data is available on file.

Cover design by Paul Qualcom
Cover photo credit iStockphoto

Print ISBN: 978-1-5107-5020-3
Ebook ISBN: 978-1-5107-5021-0

Printed in China

Contents

Disclaimer

The techniques, strategies, and suggestions expressed on the greenaislewellness.com website, courses, and coaching materials provided are intended to be used for educational purposes only. Michelle Savage and the associated Green Aisle Health & Wellness are not rendering medical advice nor are they claiming to diagnose, prescribe, or treat any disease, condition, illness, or injury.

It is imperative before beginning any nutrition or exercise program that you receive full medical clearance from a licensed physician.

Green Aisle Health & Wellness claim no responsibility to any person or entity for any liability, loss, or damage caused or alleged to be caused directly or indirectly as a result of the use, application, or interpretation of the material presented herein.

THE GREEN AISLE
HEALTH & WELLNESS

My Mission Statement

My mission as a certified integrative nutrition health coach (with specialized training in gut health) is to help those suffering from gut-related and/or weight issues to gain vibrant health and empower them to live an energized and happy life.

I support clients both in person and online via ZOOM in the comfort of their own homes, providing cutting-edge knowledge and personalized care. If desired, I also collaborate with their health-care providers so they receive the full spectrum of treatment, health education, and disease prevention information.

My mission includes providing education to increase awareness and understanding of the gut microbiome and its critical effect on health. Gut dysfunctions have resulted in an ongoing epidemic linked to many chronic diseases and conditions. These include but are not limited to candida, irritable bowel syndrome (IBS), inflammatory bowel disease (IBD), small intestinal bacterial overgrowth (SIBO), and food intolerances. Such sensitivities can result in bloating and/or pain or cramping after meals, gas, diarrhea, and/or constipation.

For some, wellness requires more than diet and lifestyle changes. Emotions play a key role in health. Clients may also need support in stress management and help to overcome depression and/or anxiety.

I support each client's path to wellness considering bio-individual and emotional needs. The goal? A healthy life of comfort, vitality, and happiness!

A Path to Vibrant Health

If you're anything like I used to be, you're thinking, *"Juice cleanse? That means I'll be starving!"* Nope—this cleanse is unique. It's a nutritional lifestyle that incorporates juicing with 80 percent raw to 20 percent cooked foods to help keep you satisfied while releasing excess weight and becoming healthier by the day. No crazy diets that leave you starving, no counting calories, no spending money on the latest weight-loss fad. You'll find that changing how you eat can be fun—as well as vital to your health!

Why do we need a cleanse? Why do we need to eat more vegetables and fruits? To counteract the environmental toxins that surround us daily and are damaging our health. Even certain foods and beverages can be detrimental. You'll learn why and much more during your journey through *The Ultimate Guide to Healthy Juicing*.

You're invited to begin your healing and revitalizing process either by following an intense 7-Day Intermittent Detox Juice Cleanse (page 43) or by easing into the 30-Day Intermittent Detox Juice Cleanse (page 51). Choose what works best for you and your body, using this book and your own intuition as your guides.

My Journey

Believe me, I wasn't always my ideal weight and free of medical issues. When I experienced digestive issues and noticed I'd outgrown my skivvies, I knew I needed to make a change. I experimented with organic juices, smoothies, and plant-based meals. My aim was to eliminate body toxins, drop the excess weight, improve my health, and boost my energy. The result? I transformed my health and my life and enjoyed using my creativity in the process!

In following my passion to become radiantly healthy and energetic, my mission became clear. I wanted to support others in attaining the health and vitality I had achieved. To that end, I became a certified integrative nutrition health coach (with training in gut health). I put my experience and knowledge into writing (three books so far—*The Green Aisle's Healthy Smoothies and Slushies* and *The Green Aisle's Healthy Indulgence*, as well as this book) and began supporting individuals on their nutritional paths.

Through this book (and coaching, if you wish, visit http://www.greenaislewellness.com/my-approach/ to learn more and schedule your consultation), I'm honored and thrilled to help you become confident in combining your own healthy menus for a vibrant new lifestyle. You'll be amazed at how you feel—and your body will thank you!

A Note about the Recipes

The detoxifying, refreshing, and innovative recipes in this book include delicious beverages, such as Superfood Tea (page 60), Grapefruit Fizz (page 61), Orange Blueberry Infusion (page 212), Immunity Juice Elixir (page 77), Mint Refresher (page 81), Celery Mint Cleanser (page 83), Ginger Shot (page 86), and many more. Can you guess what's in Tiger Nut Horchata (page 123), Monster Mash (page 79), Kingpin (page 79), Brain Teaser (page 101), or Woo Woo (page 101)? Check them out! You'll discover the perfect juice blends to perk you up in the morning and wind you down at night, as well as Happy Hour Juice Bar recipes to play with in between.

This treasure trove also provides recipes for healthy smoothies, hummus, salsa, soups, salads, and even desserts to help you feel satisfied. All the recipes are free of refined sugars, soy, corn, dairy, gluten, artificial sweeteners, and flavor enhancers, and all are plant-based. They provide active essential enzymes that stop damaging free radicals in their tracks and prevent progressive cell damage and future disease.

Make your own mylks (vegan milks, such as nut mylks), whip up a Powerhouse Breakfast Bowl (page 127) or an Deviled Chickpea Avocado Boat (page 130), or try Cashew Cream Caprese Triple-Decker (page 138) and Coconut Curry Sweet Potato Soup (page 149). You might top off your meal with a scrumptious dessert such as Sweet Tart Cheesecake (page 188) or Cantaloupe Crush Ice Pops and Soft Serve (page 195). All are *yummy treats* with satisfying and healing nutrients!

Please read the important information leading up to the recipes, as it covers a wide spectrum of related topics. For example, if you have certain diseases or illnesses, you'll want to be aware of which fruits and vegetables to avoid.

My Author's Notes (page 19) provide tips on how to prepare for your new adventure in juicing and eating and how to make the best of it to achieve fantastic results. For example, you'll discover how to wash your veggies (yes, some ways are better than others) and how and why to soak and/or sprout your nuts.

What are good plant-based sources of protein? How can you eat intuitively? Why keep a daily journal for your nutritional adventure? You'll find answers to these questions and more.

In addition, the preliminary information includes suggestions for equipment that will aid you in creating your recipes and make the process more fun. Some are optional and others, such as a juicer, are basic but with variations available. You'll read about the juicer, high-speed blender, food processor, spiralizer, immersion hand blender, and mandoline.

Coming up, we'll discuss the reasons for detoxing and benefits of juicing, and later, in the Master Juice Mixologist chapter (page 54), the art of creating your own unique juice blends.

Are you ready? Let's go!

Why Detox?

Environmental toxins surround us daily. For starters, we breathe polluted air, drink polluted water and beverages, and eat polluted food. We use polluted lotions, hair products, nail polish, soaps, household cleaning products, makeup, and perfume and ingest prescription drugs and BPAs from plastic water bottles. It seems we'd need to live in a *bubble* to achieve a completely nontoxic environment. Now is that practical—or even possible? You know the answer!

Food is Toxic? What the BLEEP!

The meat and dairy industries lead us to believe that milk does a body good and it grows strong bones. In fact, however, meat and dairy contain a hearty dose of toxins. What does a cow eat? Traditionally grass, right? Well, those cows are being fed corn and other by-products which, if not organic, are GMO foods full of Roundup weed killer!

Meat and dairy are also full of hormones and antibiotics. Recombinant bovine growth hormones (rBGH) increase the production of milk, and insulin growth factor 1 (IGF-1) promotes rapid growth in a calf. Although designed to promote cell growth and create strong bones, IGF-1 also grows unhealthy cells such as cancer cells and ages the body more quickly.

Other toxic foods include anything processed with preservatives, artificial flavors and sweeteners, corn syrup or its many counterparts, produce that's been sprayed with pesticides or other chemicals, and much more. Sadly, we just can't seem to escape toxins! They're literally harming our cells from the inside out, generating free radicals that will damage our DNA, create inflammation, and affect our health.

Digestion and Weight Loss

After consistently indulging in processed and unhealthy food, your body's digestive system becomes overworked, making it nearly impossible to fully break down and absorb all the essential enzymes and nutrients as it was designed to do. This poor digestion can create constipation, smelly or frequent gas, bloating, discomfort, and weight gain.

It sounds strange, but your bowel movements and digestion may be the best indicator of your health and ability to lose weight.

Problems with Poo?

Bowel elimination every two or three days isn't normal and can lead to a buildup of fecal matter/toxins in your intestinal tract. Ideally, you should have a bowel movement every day, with easy and quick cleanup. If you don't listen to your body and continue to eat, the toxins stay in your intestinal tract. They ferment, creating stinky gas or poo, and often lead to other health-related issues. These can include, but aren't limited to, acid reflux, IBS, heartburn, poor digestion, and even death in extreme cases of chronic constipation.

Sitting on a modern toilet at a ninety-degree angle may inhibit effective elimination of the colon. Squatting is a more natural position to eliminate. This allows the anal sphincter to open and relax. If you're experiencing constipation, using a stool or Squatty Potty can be helpful. Believe it or not, this can dramatically improve digestion, elimination, and overall health.

Detox Effects and Eliminating Toxic Foods

You may feel a little fatigue and experience headaches during a detox. These are normal reactions and they'll subside within a day or two. Consider them signs that your body is beginning to cleanse itself of toxins and celebrate!

That said, you can ease or eliminate potential detox side effects if you're willing to give the following a good, old college try. A week before the program, eliminate all fast foods, processed canned and boxed foods, GMOs, dairy, table salt, coffee, alcohol, nicotine, antibiotics, unfermented, nonorganic soy, and corn or corn-product derivatives such as high fructose corn syrup, sugar, power bars, diet shakes, white flour, white rice, soda, cookies, muffins, pastries, breads, and gluten. What's left (you might ask)? *Nutritious food!*

You can replace cow's milk with "mylks" made from almonds, hemp, oats, flax, coconut, or other nuts. Cow's milk, if nonorganic, is full of hormones and toxins.

Gluten is contained in most breads, muffins, pastries, and pastas and can damage the intestines and create what's known as a leaky gut. In turn, this can lead to obesity, diabetes, autoimmune disease, and celiac disease. Remove gluten products from your diet, and you'll see a decrease in belly fat and alleviate that bloated feeling. Now, isn't that worth the effort?

Processed foods, GMOs, coffee, alcohol, and nicotine are acidic and can easily exhaust the body. They destroy bones and deplete sodium, potassium, magnesium, and calcium, making the body prone to chronic and degenerative disease. To buffer (neutralize) the acid and safely remove it, the body "borrows" these nutrients from vital organs and bones. Not good. Over time, this strain causes the body to suffer severely, creating prolonged damage. Acid waste in the body can result in chronic fatigue, gastrointestinal diseases, diabetes, obesity, frequent colds and flu, and other health-related issues.

Once pathogens and toxins have entered the bloodstream, they're carried first to the liver and then on to other organs throughout the body. If the liver's detoxification ability is impaired due to nutritional deficiency and/or toxic overload, these toxins are stored in your fat cells. Yes, toxins are fat soluble, and when you're exposed to toxins, they make your fatty areas home base. These toxic fat cells build up year after year, creating metabolic damage that can invade vital organs such as your brain, lungs, heart, stomach, and liver, plus your bloodstream.

Known as free radicals, these toxins are damaging to the inside of the body. They destroy the enzymes essential for kidney and liver function, breathing, and digestion. Enzymes are crucial in breaking down foods and the phytic acid we consume. When the body has insufficient enzymes, the foods we eat aren't completely broken down, which causes food to sit undigested, fermenting, causing discomfort, gas, bloating, and other digestive health concerns.

Read on to discover the important reasons for giving this detox a whirl.

8 Reasons Why This Detox May Be for You!

Now you know the degree to which you've been exposed to toxins, but you may not be aware of the effects they have on you. Do you suffer from any of these problems?

1. You diet and exercise but still can't lose the weight.
2. You crave sweets, carbs, or salt.
3. You have belly fat that's hanging on for dear life!
4. You frequently feel bloated or have stinky gas or poo.
5. You have trouble falling or staying asleep.
6. You're moody or irritable.
7. You have low energy.
8. You feel scattered and can't seem to focus.

The key to weight loss and health is to flush the toxins from your fat cells. Then you'll start to see the pounds melt away and your health and vitality improve. This is where the intermittent detox juice cleanse comes into play.

Chlorophyll *(the lifeblood of a healthy diet)* from green leafy vegetables will bind to toxic substances and purge them from your body. Eating salads every day may not do the trick, as your body needs to *work* to break down necessary enzymes and nutrients, digesting slowly to metabolize them. Therefore, *concentrating your greens by juicing provides an almost intravenous purification of the blood.*

The Green Aisle Juice Fast Versus Fad Fasts

Deprivation and starvation aren't the key to losing weight, dieting, or even achieving a healthy, sustainable mind-set. Extended juice fasts can put your body in extreme shock, and if food isn't reintroduced gradually and properly, gorging after a fast can cause serious health issues.

Plus, the ingredients in a juice fast need to be combined effectively. When I first started juicing, I combined beets, carrots, and apples. *Yikes!* Because of their high glycemic index (sugar content), that combination alone will spike blood sugar, cause weight gain, and possibly lead to diabetes! Most recipe combinations in juicing programs I see online or in cleanse books have a 60/40 fruit to vegetable ratio! This is a *big* mistake when detoxing!

To the contrary, the combination of vegetable blends used in the Green Aisle Juice Bar program *will not promote diabetes* and are specifically designed to *melt away body fat*. You'll find these recipes in the Detox Juice Bar section (page 71), along with a properly designed, specific schedule for your 7-Day or 30-Day Intermittent Juice Cleanse. You can still enjoy healthy and nourishing foods, so you don't have to feel as if you're starving or feel like an emotional wreck.

Use the schedule as a guide rather than a hard-and-fast rule. As bio-individuals, what works for one person may not work for someone else. Listen to your body, and if you're struggling, feel free to add a meal from the Liquid Lunch Bar (page 143) or Snack Bar (page 133). Take advantage of the Daily Journal and Worksheet (page 38) to learn what works best for *you*. Next up, discover the benefits you'll derive from this juice fast.

"Health is like money.
We never have a true idea of its value until we lose it."
—Josh Billings

boosting
prebiotics
absorb
infection
immune
nutra
intestinal permeability
dietary
alkaline
gut
microorganisms
digs
cultures
nutrients
microbial
eat
fungus
yeast
cortisol
healing
living
heal
foods
gastrointestinal
sauerkraut
living organisms
fermented
microflora
yogurt
beneficial

tical
tract
ve enzymes
owth
kefir
supplement
intestinal living
candida
th
leaky gut
growth
healthy
friendly
flora

Benefits of a Proper Juice Fast

Short periods of juice fasting provide the body with a healthful restart and recharge. During a fast, the body's natural processes change. It clears waste from the digestive tract and releases chemicals stored in fat and other tissues and excretes them from the body.

Elimination of waste is always a good thing. Toxins take a toll on our kidneys and liver. These organs filter, break down, and remove waste from the body through the lymphatic system, lungs, skin, and colon. Fasting gives the body a break from this process while it removes excess waste. It offers an instant energy boost. When your mind doesn't have to focus on food and your body isn't focused on digesting food, you can allocate that energy to being productive in other areas.

By removing the toxins and waste buildup from your fat and tissues, you will:

- Heighten your sense of strength and happiness.
- Enhance mental clarity and focus.
- Minimize overeating and food cravings (after the first day or so).
- Improve digestive function.
- Perk up metabolism.
- Increase energy levels.
- Kick-start and enable significant weight (fat) loss.

Are you jazzed to start? Great! Please first read the next few sections. They include important health considerations, tips that will help you with the process, an explanation of equipment to consider having on hand, and instructions for the cleanse. Finally, check out your Daily Journal and Worksheet on page 38. You'll be using those during the cleanse, and you can read why it's so beneficial to keep track of your progress.

Special Considerations for Those with Disease or Illness

Please note: Not all fruits and vegetables are beneficial to everyone. For example, the Happy Hour Juice Bar recipes carry a higher glycemic load than others. (*Glycemic load* indicates how much a particular food will raise a person's blood glucose level after eating it.) Therefore, you may want to use these recipes sparingly. This is especially true if you've been diagnosed with diabetes, rheumatoid arthritis, autoimmune disease, SIBO (small intestinal bacteria overgrowth), IBS, leaky gut, gout, candidiasis, hypoglycemia, or other such illnesses for which sugar should be limited.

Likewise, if you're prone to kidney stones, it's best to avoid or limit high-oxalate vegetables, such as beets, chard, spinach, beet greens, potatoes, and nuts as well as nut mylks and chocolate.

If you have an inflammatory disease, you'll want to avoid or limit nightshade vegetables and fruits. These may worsen the symptoms of certain types of illnesses, such as autoimmune disease, lupus, rheumatoid arthritis, and other musculoskeletal pain disorders. Nightshades include tomatoes, potatoes, eggplant, peppers (cayenne, paprika, tomatillos, chiles, bell peppers), and goji berries.

Track how each food interacts with your body, mood, and symptoms using the Daily Journal and Worksheet provided right before the 7-day cleanse schedule (page 38).

Yes, drinking fresh juice is a method of treatment for disease and rejuvenating your health, but be aware of your body's sensitivities when beginning a juice fast and incorporating healthy, healing foods into your diet. Remember, it took many years to develop disease or illness, so be patient while your body slowly heals and adjusts to your new lifestyle.

Author's Notes

Whatcha Chewin'? How About Everything!

Chomp, chomp and down the hatch it goes. Yikes! We hardly chew our food. No wonder chronic digestive disorders and gastrointestinal disease are on the rise. Our saliva contains the enzyme amylase, which plays an important role in breaking down and digesting food in the mouth before it even reaches the stomach. This allows us to absorb more nutrients and maintain a healthy gut and microbiome. Fewer chews means less saliva and therefore less amylase.

Chewing "enough" takes practice! Count the number of chews you take for each bite of food. Theories abound as to how many chews are enough, but the goal is to take smaller bites and chew slowly and steadily to get your food to a liquid form before swallowing. This ensures optimum absorption and digestion. (I even chew my water and juice!)

Remember, if you've had fresh juice, brush and/or swish with water after to avoid tooth sensitivity or the need to visit your dentist.

Wash Your Veggies

Extremely important! Wash all fruits and vegetables before consuming them. They can harbor bacteria or other contaminants, such as E. coli or parasites.

Spray method: Create a homemade veggie wash made of one part white vinegar to three to four parts filtered spring water. If you like, add ¼ cup lemon juice and a bit of sea salt. Put your mixture into a spray bottle and give it a little shake.

Spray your produce and place it in a clean sink or tub, allowing it to sit for 2 to 5 minutes, all the way up to 20 minutes. Then scrub and rinse. Tap water can contain carcinogens such as arsenic and other contaminants, which can seep into your produce, so use filtered spring water for rinsing as well as spraying.

Soak method: Fill a clean sink with filtered spring water. Add 1 cup white vinegar—and lemon juice and/or a bit of sea salt, if you like. Allow the produce to sit in the sink for up to 20 minutes for a thorough cleanse; then scrub and rinse.

You'll notice after soaking that the remaining water is full of dirt and other debris. That's what you'd be consuming if you hadn't washed your fruits and veggies properly beforehand! Plus, the taste of the produce will be more pleasant after cleaning, and essential vitamins and minerals will be more readily absorbed into the body if no toxins remain.

(Plant-Based) Vegan Sources of Protein

Mom always said, "Eat your vegetables." We may have fought it at the time, but that was wise advice. Optimal health is achieved through a powerhouse plant-based diet. It isn't necessarily animal protein we crave, but the full flavor of a protein-rich meal that leaves us satiated, regardless of the protein source.

Consuming a mostly animal-based diet can tax the liver, cause inflammation, and pile on unwanted visceral abdominal fat, better known as "beer gut" or "love handles." This type of fat can lead to type 2 diabetes, insulin resistance, and many common health-related issues.

So where can you get a delicious and endless variety of protein?

Plants to the rescue! Broccoli, cauliflower, asparagus, carrots, parsnips, cabbage, apples, baby bananas, artichokes, peas, leafy greens, spinach, sprouts, watercress, spinach, kale, Brussels sprouts, collards, mustard greens, buckwheat, quinoa, oats, legumes, beans, lentils, chickpeas, walnuts, pecans, pistachios, cashews, almonds, seeds, hemp, chia, sunflower, flax, avocados, tubers, and so much more! Eat a rainbow of colors to get a complete range of nutrients and vitamins.

Don't Forget to Soak Your Nuts

Here's a tip from my book *The Green Aisle's Healthy Smoothies and Slushies* (p. 22): "It's essential to soak nuts, especially almonds, for proper digestion. Raw almonds contain tannic acid, which is an enzyme inhibitor that protects the nut until the proper environment and moisture conditions are reached to allow the nut to germinate. Eating the nut before it releases its enzyme inhibitors will make it more difficult to digest and limit nutrients your body can absorb.

"Soaking your nuts for seven to twelve hours is preferred. The next morning, drain and rinse. Presoaked nuts can be refrigerated for up to a week. Storing moist nuts may produce mold over time, so if you intend to keep the nuts as fresh as possible and keep a longer shelf life, you can dry them in a dehydrator for twelve to twenty-four hours or until crisp. If you do not have a dehydrator, you can dry them in your oven at 150 to 200 degrees until dry. Nuts are more nutritious when soaked, and, when dried, the crisp texture is scrumptious for snacking, especially when sea salt is added before the drying process."

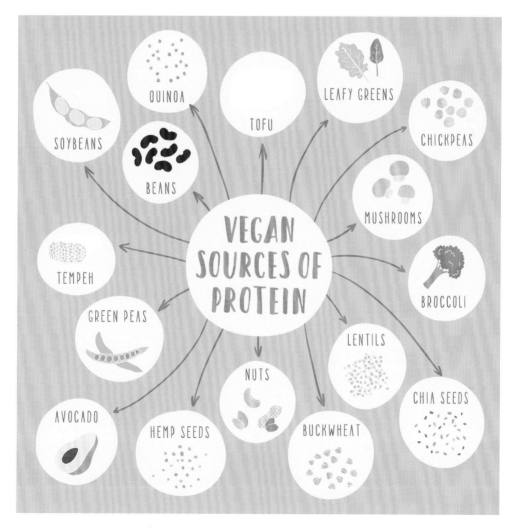

Sprouting How-To Guide

Sprouting is an act of Mother Nature's life force in germinating seeds, nuts, grains, grasses, and beans. The tender new sprouts are easily digestible and readily absorbable. Sprouting increases the absorption of B_{12}, iron, magnesium, and zinc. It makes more available concentrated vitamins and minerals, antioxidants, and enzymes, provides a larger amino acid profile, increases beneficial gut flora, and adds more soluble fiber than unsprouted.

Buy only raw, certified pathogen-free nuts, grains, grasses, and beans. If they've been irradiated, they won't sprout.

Place seeds in a quart mason jar with warm spring water, cover with cheesecloth or a sprouting screen, and soak per the following chart.

Drain and rinse and add fresh spring water at least every 12 hours to avoid mold. By 12 hours, you will see the seeds expand.

Drain and keep slightly damp by adding a bit of water. Keep uncovered and exposed to air and light to develop chlorophyll in the sprouts.

When sprouts have grown up to 2 inches long, rinse and store them in the refrigerator for up to 7 days.

Sprouts are an amazing add-in to any smoothies, soup, or salad toppings.

Sprouting Chart

Nuts	Walnuts/Pecans	Almonds	Cashews	Lentils	Oats	Mung	Alfalfa
Soak Hours	4	8	2–8	8	8	24	8
Sprout Hours	No sprouts	12	No sprout	12	48–72	48–72	48–72

Turn Juice Pulp into Creative Chow

Don't want your juice pulp to go to waste? Seal and store your vegetable pulp in the freezer. Each time you chop up your vegetables for a meal or juice, add ends of carrots, layers of onion, stems, and other snippets you would otherwise throw away to the bag of pulp in the freezer. When you have four cups or so, defrost and add it to a large saucepan of water and a bit of sea salt. Sprinkle in additional herbs or seasonings, if you like, and bring the mixture to a boil. Then reduce the heat, cover, and let the liquid and pulp simmer for a while. Strain—and voilà! You have vegetable broth.

Save a tablespoon or two of veggie pulp and sprinkle it over your salad for a nutritious topping or incorporate a bit into Raw Vegan Fudge found on page 209 or add it to soups and hummus. So many wonderful ideas to reduce waste and increase nutrition!

Extra fruit pulp? You may not want to add this to your broth, but you can add a little at a time to your smoothies when you need extra fiber. You can even press the fruit pulp into ice cube trays with a bit of water and freeze them. When you'd like to flavor a glass of water, drop in a few fruity cubes as a creative refresher. Another thought: Make a fruitful tea by boiling fruit pulp with water and adding your favorite flavors, such as a cinnamon stick or ginger root shavings, or any other herbs and spices you wish. Strain and enjoy.

Consider Serving Size

For all recipes in this book, 1 serving equals 8 ounces or less, but you may opt to eat or drink more or less, depending on your size, weight, activity level, and bio-individual need.

Feeling hungry during your intermittent detox juice cleanse? Try drinking a full glass of water first; wait 20 minutes, then reassess. You may opt to add healthy fats to your juices (see the Master Juice Mixologist chapter for more information on page 54). Many times, what you think is hunger is really thirst. Again, use your Daily Journal to keep track of when you feel hungry. Note whether you're bored, dehydrated, restless, or depressed. What's going on in your life? What emotions are coming up? This will help you recognize true hunger signs and prevent overeating. During the cleanse, when intermittently eating from the Breakfast Bar or Snack Bar, try to keep to one serving size as much as possible for better results. Eat until you are 90 percent full and wait 20 minutes before consuming water or fresh juice. This will eliminate overindulging on a cleanse. The intent is to keep the digestive system in a restful state. Such an approach will also allow for better absorption of nutrients after a meal.

Try Intuitive Eating

Do you ever find yourself lounging in front of the television munching on a bag of chips that are gone before you know it? How about driving to work in a rush with a fast-food burrito or burger in hand, hoping you don't have to slam on your brakes or perform an evasive maneuver to avoid a mess? Or, sitting down at the dinner table with your cell phone, scrolling to see who's "liked" your post rather than enjoying the company you have in the moment? Do you ever reflexively wolf down a piece of cake or a cookie without even enjoying it, then beat yourself up for it? At such times, you're disconnected from how your food feels and how it feeds and fuels your body.

Establishing a healthy, conscious relationship with food can have a huge beneficial impact on your overall health, happiness, weight, and gut flora. Slow down! Eat only when you're calm and undistracted. Contrary to what most of us do, think about what you're eating.

Repeat the following intuitive eating exercise before each meal to ensure a pleasurable experience.

Relax in your chair, hold up one bite of what you've chosen to eat, and notice its texture, temperature, color, and smell. Ask yourself:

- Where did this food come from? A farm? Where was it grown? Does it contain pesticides or is it organic? Is it from a processing facility?
- Will this food make me feel sluggish or energized?
- Will it taste amazingly delicious?
- Imagine how it will taste before it even passes your lips.
- Thank Mother Earth for this gift.
- Take a small bite and savor every flavor, chewing slowly until the food is in liquid form.
- Swallow and feel the food enter your body.
- Notice how you feel after each bite.
- Stop eating when satisfied, not full.

Establish a daily ritual of intuitive eating. Use your Daily Journal to remember what you liked or didn't like about a particular food and how it made you feel. Over time, you'll notice a shift in your relationship with food, and eating will become more pleasurable.

You are a bio-individual, so what works for another may not work for you. After your Green Aisle Juice Bar 7- or 30-Day Intermittent Detox Juice Cleanse, you can feel confident that you'll continue your journey with a sustainable healthy lifestyle.

Remember to use the Daily Journal provided to track how each food interacts with your body, mood, and symptoms, and choose recipes that work for your own bio-individual needs.

Pick up *The Green Aisle's Healthy Smoothies and Slushies* and *The Green Aisle's Healthy Indulgence.* Finally, you can indulge without guilt and never worry about what's for dinner. These recipes incorporate the simplest, freshest, non-GMO, organic foods you can get your hands on. The ingredients are combined so artfully and deliciously that you'll be hooked on health!

Suggested Equipment List

Some women are obsessed with buying shoes or purses or shopping in general. Me? I love kitchen appliances! I don't mind paying a pretty penny for them because I spend most of my day in the kitchen using them. When I'm in the kitchen whippin' up creative dishes, I'm in my Zen. Although I use and recommend the equipment listed, you needn't purchase these particular items or brands to create any of the recipes. If you're on a budget and don't have a juicer but want to try juicing or start the cleanse, you can blend all the veggies in a traditional blender along with approximately one cup of water. Blend until smooth and strain through a fine mesh strainer or using a rubber spatula to press it through into a bowl, or you can squeeze it through cheesecloth. Easy peasy!

Juicers

All recipes in this book have been created using my masticating Omega VRT350 vertical single-auger low-speed widemouthed juicer. Wow—that's a mouthful! But never mind the name; this juicer is amazing!

Following is "The Juicer Lowdown," written by my beautiful friend Melissa Kubek, owner of Organic Cold-Pressed Juice & Plant-Based Eats in Canada. Melissa will help you determine which juicer is best for you.

The Juicer Lowdown *by Melissa Kubek*
Centrifugal Juicer vs. Masticating Juicer vs. Cold-pressed Juicer

Several years ago, when I began my juicing journey, prior to juicing being as mainstream and trendy as it is now, I felt as though there were no clear-cut answers to the questions that I had about it. At the time, I was going through a few major life shifts and I was looking for a way to detoxify my body, lose a little weight, and get my body back to a healthy state. I happened to stumble upon a 5-to7-day detox program based around homemade juice. I knew nothing about juicing and yet I had been a strong advocate for natural health, organic foods and veganism since my early twenties. I believed at the time that drinking smoothies and eating fruits and vegetables were the best way to promote health in the body because the only juices that I was familiar with were the shelf-stable Tetra Paks (juice boxes, apple juice, etc. . . .), concentrated juices in the freezer section of the grocery store or the refrigerated varieties. To me, at the time, grocery store juice was an alternative to the sugar-laden sodas and I didn't understand how juice could possibly heal my body as the home juicing enthusiasts were promoting.

I am an extreme researcher with a passion for biology and genetics. I sought out any and all information that I could find regarding home juicing, and within a short period of time, not only was my mind completely blown away by what I had uncovered, but my body was also rapidly changing in more positive ways than I could have imagined, especially as I increased my daily intake of my homemade juice.

The quick version of what I learned is this—juicing, in my opinion, is the easiest way to deliver potent live nutrients (aka your body's building blocks) in large quantities when it's done correctly. Homemade juice can be a powerful resource for restoring health to the body overall. In this section I'm going to break down my years of research into a few points regarding juicing basics so that you can make the most of your juicing experience. You're going to learn about why juicing is a superior vehicle for delivering nutrients to the bloodstream and you'll learn the differences among the three main types of home juicers.

So, what is juicing? There are many misconceptions about what juicing is. In order to answer the question "What is juicing?" we need to take a quick look at your body, more specifically your digestive system.

When we eat food or drink smoothies, our bodies undergo a process to extract the nutrients away from the bulk of the food and break down these nutrients into smaller particles in order to hopefully be absorbed and utilized by the body. This process is metabolically expensive, meaning the body requires massive amounts of energy to complete the process. This is where juicing comes in handy. A juicer is able to complete this initial extraction process on the body's behalf, thereby allowing the body to utilize its energy toward healing, detoxifying and strengthening.

When we consume this type of juice, the vast majority of the nutrients end up in the bloodstream. Whereas when we consume solid foods or mulched/masticated/pre-chewed foods (aka smoothies, blended foods) we risk losing many of these nutrients due to being burned up during the digestion process as well as losing those nutrients that ultimately end up reattaching to the fiber or other food bulk while in the small intestine.

The bottom line is this: for every 2 pounds of produced juiced (yielding approximately 400ml of juice), we would need to consume by eating or blending (smoothies) approximately 6 to 8 pounds of produce in order to absorb the same quantity of nutrients. The vast majority of us wouldn't eat 6 to 8 pounds of produce in a single sitting, but most of us could easily drink 400 ml of juice.

Now that you have a basic understanding of why juicing is the way to go when you're wanting to heal, detoxify and strengthen your body, let's talk about the three main types of home juicers. Not all juicers are equal! Each juicer type offers their own set of pros and cons. We'll review each of these types using the following criteria: ease of use, extraction method, juice yield, nutrient yield, and price point.

The Centrifugal Juicer

These are the most common juicers used in homes and in commercial juice/smoothie bars. They are fast, very loud, easy to assemble, easy to clean, and don't require much in the way of maintenance. At the heart of the centrifugal juicer is the blade basket. This is a flat-bottomed fine mesh basket typically with two blades for cutting produce at the base. These centrifugal juicers extract using centrifugal force by spinning at speeds of 15,000 RPM. Produce is typically fed through a relatively wide opening at the top of the machine where it will drop down (or be pushed down using the provided tamp) into the blade basket. The blade basket will very quickly chop the produce, and the centrifugal force will pull the liquid through the fine mesh, where it will exit the juicer via the juice spout, while at the same time, the still fairly wet pulp is ejected into the pulp bin (typically attached to the juicer).

This extraction method is very fast and very easy to do, and therefore the centrifugal juicer is the best of the juicers to use at the beginning of your juicing journey. There is very minimal produce preparation required, it's easy to set up, easy to clean, and offers very fast extraction. I highly recommend, however, as soon as you are familiar with juicing and you've made it a part of your daily life, switch to a masticating juicer. The downside of centrifugal juicers is that they are centrifugal juicers. What I mean by this is that their extraction method causes rapid degeneration of the nutrients and a cascade of oxidative reactions throughout the live nutrients in the juice.

Simply put, by using centrifugal force at such fast speeds, nearly 95 percent of the nutrients will be dead, oxidized, or disabled by the time you drink your fresh made juice. Furthermore, you'll only have approximately 15 minutes with the remaining 5 percent of live nutrients before those too are degraded and oxidized, therefore this juice cannot be stored. From a health and healing standpoint, these juicers cause more negative effects than positive ones; however, from the standpoint of ease of use, these are by far the best and easiest juicers to get started with. Just be sure to move on to a masticating juicer as soon as you feel comfortable with the juicing process and have made it a daily habit in your life. You will feel some benefits from the juice extracted by these centrifugal juicers, especially if you don't consume many raw fruits and veggies every day.

Price-wise these juicers are the least expensive of the bunch and range between $25 (used) to $500 brand new. My suggestion is to purchase a used centrifugal juicer to learn on and then spend your money on a masticating juicer when you're ready to step up your juicing game.

The Masticating Juicer

Get ready to spend some time! These juicers require a fair amount of produce prep in the way of chopping fruits and vegetables (especially leafy greens). The extraction method is similar to the centrifugal juicers in that there is a single opening at the top of the juicer; there is a spout for the extracted liquids and a spout for the pulp. The actual method of extraction, however, is very different. Instead of a high-speed chopping basket, they utilize a single or double slow grinding auger system.

Produce is fed into the mouth of the juicer very slowly. The auger(s) will typically pull the produce slowly into the juicer and grind the produce down into a fine mushy pulp, ultimately moving through a fine metal screen where the liquid falls through into a container placed below the juice spout, and the pulp is pushed through a small hole leading to a pulp holding container.

The masticating juicers are slow with a fairly labor-intensive process, unlike their centrifugal counterparts. The masticating juicers also come with many more parts to clean and are a little more complex to assemble than the centrifugal juicers. In my opinion, however, the immense benefits of masticated juice completely outweigh any possible negatives.

Benefit #1: The masticating augers spin at only 40–120 RPM. This means that the vast majority of the extracted nutrients remain intact and viable! Keep in mind that unless you are growing your own organic produce, it can be somewhat expensive to purchase. Therefore, when you are juicing your produce, a key component to pay attention to in addition to fluid yield is nutrient yield. Unlike the centrifugal's 5 percent nutrient yield and 15-minute shelf life, the masticating juicer can retain 30 to 50 percent of the live nutrients for up to 48 hours when quickly contained, airtight sealed, and refrigerated. (Never freeze your juice if nutrient yield is important to you. Freezing will cause the cell walls to burst, thereby killing off the live components of the juice).

Next to a cold-pressed juicer, the masticating juicer is the best for home use. The juice extracted from these juicers have the ability (when done correctly) to heal, detoxify, and strengthen our bodies. They also produce a much dryer pulp than that of the centrifugal juicers. This means that a greater level of extraction is taking place with the masticating juicer, thereby offering a better bang for your buck when it comes to the cost of purchasing organic produce.

While these juicers are more labor intensive, are more work to clean up, and take longer overall, they have the ability to produce a powerful and nutrient-rich juice. You would need to consume approximately ten cups of the centrifugal juice in order to consume the same level of nutrients from one cup of masticated juice. These juicers also cost far more than the centrifugal juicers and can range between $125 used to $2,000 new. Due to their slightly higher maintenance requirements and slow extraction, masticating juicers are typically only found in homes and not in juice bars.

There are some juice companies that claim to offer cold-pressed juice (we'll dive into cold-pressed in a moment) or fresh pressed juice, however they are using either a centrifugal juicer or masticating juicer for their extraction process. Centrifugal and masticating juicers are NOT capable of cold-pressed extraction, and therefore when a company or juice bar is claiming they sell cold-pressed juice or fresh pressed juice, please find out what type of extractor/juicer they are using prior to purchasing your juice. If they are using a centrifugal or masticating juicer, you know that their juice is not cold-pressed and not as nutrient dense as they are claiming.

The Cold-Pressed Juicer

The cold-pressed juicer is the king of all juicers and the ultimate of extraction methods. It's also the most labor intensive, requires the most cleanup and ranges in price from $2,300 to $5,000 USD for the home version. They are rarely available for purchase as used units. Commercial cold-pressed juicers range from $18,000 USD for a countertop unit to over $100,000 for the larger presses.

The cold-pressed process is twofold: 1. The produce is mulched into a chunky applesauce pulp; 2. The pulp is placed into a mesh bag or cloth which is then inserted into a stainless steel press where the liquid is extracted typically using hydraulic pressure. As there is no spinning or rotating used to extract the nutrients (which causes the slight heating and denaturing of nutrients), this is a cold method of extraction. The use of the hydraulic press is the other part of the equation. The cold-pressed extraction is a highly unique process! Unlike the centrifugal and masticating juicers, the home cold-pressed juicer is rectangular in shape and typically comes equipped with several different grinder options, depending upon the produce being juiced, as well as juice cloths/bags, food-grade hydraulic fluid, spare parts and tools, etc.

The juice that comes from this type of extraction method is extremely potent, the plant cells, beneficial bacteria, enzymes, phytonutrients, and plant DNA for most part are viable and fully intact. Nearly 100 percent of the nutrients are available for absorption by the body, and the juice can last for up to five days providing the juice was made in a cool environment, using organic produce that was properly prepared, and then immediately properly airtight sealed and stored in a refrigerator.

In regards to extraction yield, the cold-pressed juicer is untouchable and can yield between 30 and 80 percent more juice than the same amount of produce juiced by a masticating juicer. If you plan on making juicing part of your lifestyle, you will likely want to invest in a cold-pressed juicer after some time with your masticating juicer as you will save on the cost of produce by nearly half!

A clarification that needs to be made here is that of cold-pressed juiced and cold pressure processed. These are two very distinct processes, and in my opinion, labeling a juice as cold pressured or cold pressure processed is very misleading to the general consumer who believes that this means they are purchasing cold-pressed juice. CPP (cold pressure processing), also known as HPP (high-pressure processing) is a secondary treatment that some commercially sold cold-pressed juices undergo in order to artificially extend their shelf life from a maximum of 5 days to a maximum of 30 to 45 days. The quick version of this process, is that a pressure with the equivalent to more than the pressure found in the deepest part of the ocean (the Mariana Trench) is applied uniformly to the sealed juice bottles, thereby obliterating anything in the juice that may be live, such as bacteria (which can have incredible benefits to our immune system and overall well-being), enzymes (specialized proteins that are injured during this process by forcing them to unfold unnaturally), and more. The incredibly live and potent cold-pressed juice is now dead and won't provide you with the benefits of live, raw cold-pressed juice. Look for cold pressure processed or HPP on the labels of your juice or simply look at the "best before" date. If it's any more than a few days away, you can be sure that the juice has undergone additional processing to artificially extend its shelf life, and you shouldn't pay any more than what you would typically pay for a bottle of store-bought orange juice.

A final important note to make about juicing is that organic produce should be the only produce that makes its way through your juicer! Keep in mind these are extractors and they don't differentiate between nutrients and toxins (aka pesticides). My understanding from most of the individuals I have coached and spoken with in regard to juicing is that they believe if they simply wash the skin on their nonorganic produce or peel it, that it's enough to get rid of any pesticides. This is a massive misconception.

Conventional produce begins typically with a seed that is either a genetically modified version of its original self and/or it contains a built-in pesticide (and often a built-in antibiotic). Over the course of the conventionally grown plant's life, it will have not only begun from a toxic altered seed, but it will have been planted in nutritionally inferior and toxic soil and then consistently sprayed with toxins over the course of its life. Being extremely porous, these plants are saturated with toxins! Pesticides are pulled into the plants from their root systems and absorbed topically. The glyphosate and other chemicals are not on the surface of the plant in a washable form, they are the plant. They are the seed, the flesh, and the skin, and they taste different from organic plants.

When these toxic plants are running through a juice extractor, not only are the limited available nutrients from the plants extracted, but the pesticides are also extracted. You are then left with a toxic drink that has the ability to hit the bloodstream within 6 minutes of consumption. This is especially the case with cold-pressed juice. As this method of extraction is far superior to the others, it also means that if your juice has been made with conventional produce using cold-pressed extraction, that you may be poisoning your body instead of healing it. *Always and only* ever use *organic* produce when juicing! When purchasing juice from a store, ensure that it has been made using 100 percent organic produce by cold-pressed extraction method and that it has a refrigerated shelf life of minimally 3 days to a maximum of 5 days. In order for juice to contain maximum nutrient potency, it must check off all 3 of those boxes.

I'm excited for you and your juicing journey ahead! Remember to have patience throughout this process, have fun, feel healthy, and get creative with your juices. Find or create recipes that you'll love and will be easy for you to do daily. As I've stated already, as you begin this journey I highly recommend starting with a centrifugal juicer as a way to "get your feet wet," and, as soon as you're ready, move up to a masticating juicer. For your body's basic nutrient needs, a masticating juicer will do a brilliant job and may be all you'll ever need. However, for deeper healing or disease treatment, a cold-pressed juicer is required in addition to the sound advice of your trusted natural health care practitioner.

Happy juicing,

Melissa Kubek
www.litebod.com
Organic Cold-Pressed Juice & Plant-Based Eats
Litebod Juice Co.
#7-33039 1st Ave
Mission, B.C. Canada

High-Speed Blender

As we discussed in *The Green Aisle's Healthy Smoothies and Slushies*, a high-speed blender is a must-have in the kitchen and highly recommended for creating top-notch, restaurant-style smoothies and improving your health.

My two all-time favorites are the Blendtec (which I use) and Vitamix. These bad boys are all-in-one, high-speed blenders that not only make creamy fruit and veggie smoothies, but also nut butters, dips, dressings, nut mylks, sauces, baby food, ice cream, creamy soups, and much more.

When you put your favorite ingredients into the blender, it automatically speeds up and slows down, then shuts off when the cycle is complete. This way, your smoothie recipes turn out perfect every time—in only 40 seconds. With its user-friendly design, cleanup is quick and easy. The blender also fits easily under most cabinetry.

Food Processor

After purchasing my beautiful Empire Red KitchenAid 12-cup food processor, I've never gone back to spending hours chopping, grating, or mixing large batches of vegetables.

Onions used to be my nemesis as they made my mascara run. When I chopped them, I looked like a funny racoon in no time. I now pop those eye-watering pups right into my food processor—and no raccoon!

The widemouthed feed tube of my processor accommodates large items such as tomatoes, cucumbers, and potatoes with minimal prep beforehand. My kids love my Cast-Iron Potato Pie. Instead of shredding the potatoes forever, I just plop roughly chopped pieces into the food processor, set it on high, and let it run for less than a minute. It's magic! (I told you I get excited over my kitchen appliances!)

Spiralizer

After returning from a splendid San Diego mini-vacation with my juicing sistas, my friend Kaz Bee surprised me with a spiralizer. I was using hers on the trip and always wanted one. She loved the raw vegan meals I created during our vacation so much she decided to give me this delightful gift. Was I ever excited! It almost felt like Christmas morning!

Trimming the waistline was all the more joyful now that I could play with my spiralizer. I could have oodles of fun making veggie pasta and delectable crispy baked curly fries (just drizzle with olive oil, season generously with sea salt and other spices, and bake at 425 degrees for 20 to 30 minutes). And picture this: an Asian sesame salad with spiralized cucumbers and carrots tossed in a tongue-pleasing infusion of rice vinegar, maple syrup or honey, lime juice, toasted sesame oil, black sesame seeds, and cilantro. Oh *yum!*

Immersion Hand Blender

Sometimes I want to puree directly in the pot, and I found the perfect tool to do it. For the Liquid Lunch Bar, I've cut down my prep and cleaning times by using the Cuisinart Smart Stick Immersion Hand Blender. The long handle reaches easily into pots, pitchers, and bowls, and it has a whisk attachment option and an easy one-touch control. Plus, it's dishwasher safe, which makes for easy cleanup. I'm lovin' it!

Mandoline

What's a mandoline, you may ask? It's a tool for making nice neat slices. Want to make uniform onion slices while minimizing and possibly avoiding the raccoon eyes I mentioned earlier? The mandoline can quickly slice those tearjerking onions, making prep time a snap. You can also use it to julienne vegetables, making small matchstick-size strips of, say, carrots or zucchini. I use my Cuisinart mandoline for perfectly sliced tomatoes, too. Perfect for my Cashew Cream Caprese Triple-Decker salad found on page 138, it provides adjustable slicing width, is dishwasher safe, and includes storage for featured blades. Another wonderful kitchen toy!

How to Perform the Intermittent Detox Juice Cleanse

The Green Aisle's Intermittent Detox Juice Cleanse includes a 7-day and a 30-day schedule with designated Juice Bars from which to choose. The 7-day cleanse is perfect for those who want to jump in with two feet—a more intense and restrictive schedule for juicing enthusiasts. The 30-day cleanse is great for those who are a bit hesitant to commit or whose lifestyles can't support the shorter approach. It gently eases you into a healthier lifestyle, strategically designed to improve your health gradually with lasting results and a plan you will stick to for many years to come. The Green Aisle's Juice Bar includes meal plans complete with recipes for both juices and light snacks and meals for whichever cleanse you choose.

Pre-Cleanse Instructions

Eliminate any unforeseen hiccups in your cleanse by prepping ahead of time. Choose which cleanse will work best for your bio-individual needs and read the schedule thoroughly. Choose which meals or juices you would love to make one week at a time. Prepare your produce and store it in individual containers so you can grab what you need without fuss. This will keep you on track to success.

Time permitting, clear out all the junk and clutter from your refrigerator and cupboards, and clean your kitchen as if you were going to showcase it. Seeing a bag of chips or cookies may be tempting and throw you off track. Having healthy snacks in view will eliminate unhealthy temptations and enjoying your beautifully clean kitchen will lessen any anxiety.

A cleanse isn't just about weight loss and eating clean, healthy food for physical vitality and balance. It's about becoming balanced in all areas of your life, including mental, emotional, and spiritual. Nourish yourself in all areas of your life!

Now that you're prepared for your cleanse, let's look at the Daily Journal and Worksheet and why you'll want to use them. Then choose your cleanse and enjoy your new adventure in healthy eating!

Daily Journal and Worksheet

It's important to record how everything you ingest affects you physically, mentally, and emotionally. This can help you pinpoint possible food allergens and/or sensitivities. It can also help you uncover how your feelings affect your eating habits and may trigger overeating. Do you eat when you're bored, angry, sad, frustrated, tired, or lonely? Note what's going on in your life and how it correlates with your eating.

Note that during the first few days of a detox you may have uncomfortable symptoms, but as the days progress, you'll see improvements in your overall energy and happiness.

You can copy the following templates for your Daily Journal and Worksheet to record details of how you feel, keep you on track, and celebrate your progress.

DAILY JOURNAL

When food no longer controls you, you can observe your thoughts, emotions, and pleasure around it without judgment, guilt, or shame. ~ Health Coach Michelle Savage

DAY: _____ **DATE:** _____

_____
_____
_____
_____
_____
_____
_____
_____
_____
_____
_____
_____
_____
_____
_____
_____
_____
_____
_____
_____
_____
_____

DAY: _____ **DATE:** _____

Describe what you had to eat or what you did for exercise, how you felt physically, mentally, emotionally, and any life event that was affecting you.

Wake-Up: _____

_____

Breakfast: _____

_____

Snack: _____

_____

Lunch: _____

_____

Snack: _____

_____

Dinner: _____

_____

Bedtime: _____

_____

Water: _____oz. Exercise: _____

DAY: _____ **DATE:** _____

Describe what you had to eat or what you did for exercise,
how you felt physically, mentally, emotionally, and any life
event that was affecting you.

Wake-Up: _____

_____

Breakfast: _____

_____

Snack: _____

_____

Lunch: _____

_____

Snack: _____

_____

Dinner: _____

_____

Bedtime: _____

_____

Water: _____oz. Exercise: _____

7-Day Intermittent Detox Juice Cleanse Schedule

Day 1
Wake-Up:	8 oz. water, Morning Juice Bar
Breakfast:	8 oz. water, Detox Juice Bar
Snack:	8 oz. water, Detox Juice Bar
Lunch:	8 oz. water, Detox Juice Bar

30-minute light exercise: yoga, stretching, or brisk walking

Snack:	8 oz. water, Detox Juice Bar
Dinner:	8 oz. water, Detox Juice Bar
Bedtime:	8 oz. water, Last Call

Day 2
Wake-Up:	8 oz. water, Morning Juice Bar
Breakfast:	8 oz. water, Detox Juice Bar
Snack:	8 oz. water, Detox Juice Bar
Lunch:	8 oz. water, Detox Juice Bar or Liquid Lunch Bar

30-minute light exercise: yoga, stretching, or brisk walking

Snack:	8 oz. water, Detox Juice Bar
Dinner:	8 oz. water, Detox Juice Bar or Liquid Lunch Bar
Bedtime:	8 oz. water, Last Call

Day 3
Wake-Up:	8 oz. water, Morning Juice Bar
Breakfast:	8 oz. water, Detox Juice Bar or Smoothie Bar
Snack:	8 oz. water, Detox Juice Bar
Lunch:	8 oz. water, Liquid Lunch Bar

30-minute light exercise: yoga, stretching, or brisk walking

Snack:	8 oz. water, Detox Juice Bar or Snack Bar
Dinner:	8 oz. water, Detox Juice Bar or Liquid Lunch Bar
Bedtime:	8 oz. water, Last Call

Day 4

Wake-Up:	8 oz. water, Morning Juice Bar
Breakfast:	8 oz. water, Detox Juice Bar or Smoothie Bar
Snack:	8 oz. water, Detox Juice Bar or Snack Bar
Lunch:	8 oz. water, Liquid Lunch Bar

30-minute light exercise: yoga, stretching, or walking

Snack:	8 oz. water, Detox Juice Bar
Dinner:	8 oz. water, Liquid Lunch Bar or Salad Bar
Bedtime:	8 oz. water, Last Call

Day 5

Wake-Up:	8 oz. water, Morning Juice Bar or Smoothie Bar
Breakfast:	8 oz. water, Breakfast Bar
Snack:	8 oz. water, Detox Juice Bar or Smoothie Bar
Lunch:	8 oz. water, Liquid Lunch Bar

30-minute light exercise: yoga, stretching, or brisk walking

Snack:	8 oz. water, Detox Juice Bar
Dinner:	8 oz. water, Liquid Lunch Bar or Salad Bar
Bedtime:	8 oz. water, Last Call

Day 6

Wake-Up:	8 oz. water, Morning Juice Bar or Smoothie Bar
Breakfast:	8 oz. water, Breakfast Bar
Snack:	8 oz. water, Snack Bar
Lunch:	8 oz. water, Liquid Lunch Bar or Salad Bar

30-minute moderate exercise: yoga, stretching, or brisk walking

Snack:	8 oz. water, Detox Juice Bar
Dinner:	8 oz. water, Post-Cleanse Bar or Salad Bar
Bedtime:	8 oz. water, Last Call

Day 7

Wake-Up:	8 oz. water, Morning Juice Bar or Smoothie Bar
Breakfast:	8 oz. water, Breakfast Bar
Snack:	8 oz. water, Detox Juice Bar or Snack Bar
Lunch:	8 oz. water, Liquid Lunch Bar or Salad Bar

30-minute moderate exercise: yoga, stretching, or brisk walking

Snack:	8 oz. water, Detox Juice Bar
Dinner:	8 oz. water, Post-Cleanse Bar or Salad Bar
Bedtime:	8 oz. water, Dessert Bar, Last Call

You made it! Congratulations! You've accomplished a lot, and I bet you feel amazing!

Now it's time to gently return to more solid foods. If you like, you can continue on with the 30-Day Intermittent Detox Juice Cleanse (page 51) to ease yourself further into health and vibrancy. Otherwise, you may choose to complete your cleanse here and incorporate more complex foods into your diet. Be sure to continue drinking plenty of water, eat your greens, chew thoroughly, and be gentle with yourself. Take it slow.

Looking for healthy recipes now that you're feeling energized? Pick up a copy of my cookbook, *The Green Aisle's Healthy Indulgence*. These recipes combine the finest organic, seasonal produce with other mouthwatering ingredients. Indulge in appealing and satisfying meals inspired by locations and cuisines around the world.

Remember the dedication you put into your cleanse. Reread your Daily Journal to remind yourself of what you learned and reflect on your journey.

Meet My Happy Clients

Sarah Ferrucci, Age 33, Benicia, California
Sarah decided she loved the results of the 7-day cleanse so much she *hired* me for the next 30 days! She was a *beast*—prepping her juices for work, exercising 5 days a week, and doing the work!

I was looking to make a change in my life and this program gave me exactly what I was looking for. It gave me energy, nutritional education, weight loss, and most importantly confidence to be the me I wanted to be!

Watch Sarah's transformation video!
http://www.greenaislewellness.com/testimonials/

Day 1
Left Arm: **11.75in**
Chest: **39.75in**
High Waist: **34in**
Belly Button: **36.25in**
Lower Waist: **36in**
Hips: **39.75in**
Left Thigh: **24in**
Weight: **174lbs**

Day 30
Left Arm: **11in**
Chest: **37in**
High Waist: **31in**
Belly Button: **34in**
Lower Waist: **36in**
Hips: **37.5in**
Left Thigh: **22in**
Weight: **161lbs**

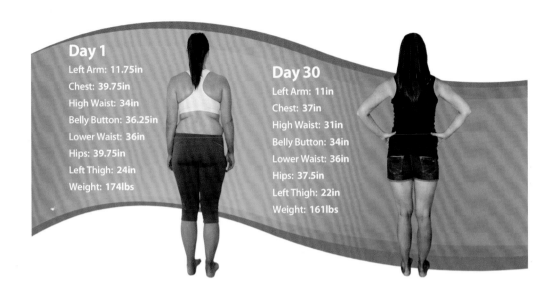

Day 1
Left Arm: **11.75in**
Chest: **39.75in**
High Waist: **34in**
Belly Button: **36.25in**
Lower Waist: **36in**
Hips: **39.75in**
Left Thigh: **24in**
Weight: **174lbs**

Day 30
Left Arm: **11in**
Chest: **37in**
High Waist: **31in**
Belly Button: **34in**
Lower Waist: **36in**
Hips: **37.5in**
Left Thigh: **22in**
Weight: **161lbs**

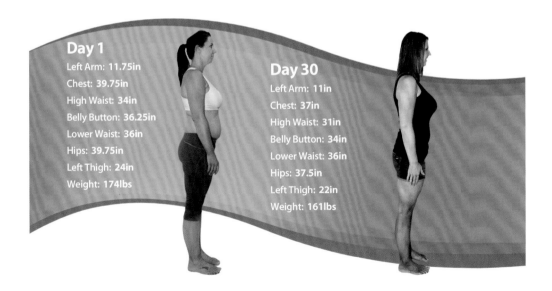

Day 1
Left Arm: **11.75in**
Chest: **39.75in**
High Waist: **34in**
Belly Button: **36.25in**
Lower Waist: **36in**
Hips: **39.75in**
Left Thigh: **24in**
Weight: **174lbs**

Day 30
Left Arm: **11in**
Chest: **37in**
High Waist: **31in**
Belly Button: **34in**
Lower Waist: **36in**
Hips: **37.5in**
Left Thigh: **22in**
Weight: **161lbs**

Janica Larson, Age 31, Albany, Minnesota
Simply Living with Janica—https://www.janicalarson.com/
Certified Holistic Health Coach and Online Business Coach for Health Conscious Mompreneurs

This 7-day cleanse helped me in SO many ways! Not only did I lose 4 pounds and 6 ½ inches, I was able to change a lot of my daily habits permanently, including cutting back on sugar and caffeine.

On top of the actual program, which is laid out in a super easy to implement way, the support I received from Michelle was stellar! She checked in on me and was available to answer questions when I felt like I was struggling. I also want to add that the way she has this cleanse set up, there was minimal struggle! The knowledge base and the way things are organized keeps it so easy and makes doing the cleanse a fun adventure!

I was still nursing my daughter when I did this, so Michelle gave me the go-ahead to have a few extra healthy-fat snacks to keep me going, and my milk supply actually went up!

I ended the cleanse feeling proud of my accomplishment, full of energy, and actually planning the next round. I am just about a week away from my second session, and I am super confident that I will have the same results.

7 Day Detox
Results!

4 pounds & 6 1/2 inches lost!

Day 1
135 pounds
236.5 inches

Day 7
131 pounds
230 inches

janicalarson.com

Janica has lived a healthy, mindful lifestyle since 2011 when her dad was diagnosed with congestive heart failure. It was then she knew she and her family needed to make some big changes. After quitting smoking and losing over 40 pounds, she decided to become a health coach so she could teach others to take their health seriously too. After learning how to run a successful business, she started coaching other health coaches. Janica realized the way she could get her healthy message to the most amount of people was to help other health-conscious people get their work into the world. Today she is serving mompreneurs all over the world to help them create the business of their dreams by giving them the tools to do it on *their* terms!

Meet more happy clients on page 224.

30-Day Intermittent Detox Juice Cleanse Schedule

Days 1–3

Wake-Up:	8 oz. water, Morning Juice Bar or Smoothie Bar
Breakfast:	8 oz. water, Breakfast Bar
Snack:	8 oz. water, Detox Juice Bar or Snack Bar
Lunch:	8 oz. water, Liquid Lunch Bar or Salad Bar

30-minute moderate exercise: yoga, stretching, or brisk walking

Snack:	8 oz. water, Detox Juice Bar or Snack Bar
Dinner:	8 oz. water, Post-Cleanse Bar or Salad Bar
Bedtime:	8 oz. water, Dessert Bar and Last Call

Days 4–7

Wake-Up:	8 oz. water, Morning Juice Bar or Smoothie Bar
Breakfast:	8 oz. water, Breakfast Bar
Snack:	8 oz. water, Detox Juice Bar
Lunch:	8 oz. water, Liquid Lunch Bar

30-minute light exercise: yoga, stretching, or brisk walking

Snack:	8 oz. water, Detox Juice Bar
Dinner:	8 oz. water, Liquid Lunch or Salad Bar
Bedtime:	8 oz. water, Last Call

Days 8–10

Wake-Up:	8 oz. water, Morning Juice Bar
Breakfast:	8 oz. water, Detox Juice Bar or Smoothie Bar
Snack:	8 oz. water, Detox Juice Bar
Lunch:	8 oz. water, Detox Juice Bar or Liquid Lunch Bar

30-minute light exercise: yoga, stretching, or brisk walking

Snack:	8 oz. water, Detox Juice Bar
Dinner:	8 oz. water, Detox Juice Bar or Liquid Lunch Bar
Bedtime:	8 oz. water, Last Call

Days 11–14

Wake-Up:	8 oz. water, Morning Juice Bar or Smoothie Bar
Breakfast:	8 oz. water, Breakfast Bar
Snack:	8 oz. water, Detox Juice Bar
Lunch:	8 oz. water, Salad Bar

30-minute light exercise: yoga, stretching, or brisk walking

Snack:	8 oz. water, Detox Juice Bar or Snack Bar
Dinner:	8 oz. water, Liquid Lunch or Salad Bar
Bedtime:	8 oz. water, Last Call

Days 15–18

Wake-Up:	8 oz. water, Morning Juice Bar or Smoothie Bar
Breakfast:	8 oz. water, Breakfast Bar
Snack:	8 oz. water, Snack Bar
Lunch:	8 oz. water, Liquid Lunch Bar or Salad Bar

30-minute moderate exercise: yoga, stretching, or brisk walking

Snack:	8 oz. water, Detox Juice Bar
Dinner:	8 oz. water, Post-Cleanse Bar or Salad Bar
Bedtime:	8 oz. water, Dessert Bar, Last Call

Days 19–22

Wake-Up:	8 oz. water, Morning Juice Bar or Smoothie Bar
Breakfast:	8 oz. water, Breakfast Bar
Snack:	8 oz. water, Snack Bar and/or Mylk Bar
Lunch:	8 oz. water, Liquid Lunch Bar or Salad Bar

30-minute moderate exercise: yoga, stretching, or brisk walking

Snack:	8 oz. water, Detox Juice Bar
Dinner:	8 oz. water, Post-Cleanse Bar or Salad Bar
Bedtime:	8 oz. water, Dessert Bar and/or Mylk Bar, Last Call

Wake-Up:	8 oz. water, Morning Juice Bar or Smoothie Bar
Breakfast:	8 oz. water, Breakfast Bar
Snack:	8 oz. water, Snack Bar and Mylk Bar
Lunch:	8 oz. water, Salad Bar

30-minute moderate exercise: yoga, stretching, or brisk walking

Snack:	8 oz. water, Snack Bar and Mylk Bar
Dinner:	8 oz. water, Post-Cleanse Bar
Bedtime:	8 oz. water, Dessert Bar and Mylk Bar, Last Call

Be proud of yourself! You've transitioned into a healthy lifestyle with enriching and nourishing food! If at this point you'd like to transition into a more whole-foods approach, continue on to **Days 27–30** for some special bonus recipes!

On the other hand, if you wish to shed a few more pounds, you can repeat the 30-Day Intermittent Detox Juice Cleanse or dive back into the 7-Day Intermittent Detox Juice Cleanse, a formula that provides maximum results in a shorter duration. Listen to your body; remember what works for one bio-individual may not work for another. Choose whichever schedule will work best for the results you'd like right now.

After that, pick up *The Green Aisle's Healthy Indulgence* cookbook. You'll be inspired by the amazingly healthy and delicious recipes from around the world and never have to wonder what's for dinner—or any other meal for that matter!

Days 27–30 Special Bonus Recipes see page 197

Wake-Up:	8 oz. water, Morning Juice Bar or Smoothie Bar
Breakfast:	8 oz. water, Overnight Oats and Detox Juice Bar or Cast-Iron Potato Pie and Detox Juice Bar or Coconut Cream Cheese Fruit Rice Cake and Smoothie Bar (great options to choose from..)
Snack:	8 oz. water, Snack Bar and Mylk Bar
Lunch:	8 oz. water, Tomato Basil Gazpacho or Quinoa Tabbouli Salad

30-minute moderate exercise: yoga, stretching, or brisk walking

Snack:	8 oz. water, Happy Hour Juice Bar or Snack Bar
Dinner:	8 oz. water, Jade Pearl Rice Ramen or 10-Minute Veggie Stir Fry
Bedtime:	8 oz. water, Raw Vegan Fudge or Coconut Cream Cheese Fruit Rice Cake

Master Juice Mixologist

Learn the art of creating your own unique juice blends by properly combining produce to support your health and pique your taste buds. This element of personal creativity will make your new healthy living more delicious, enjoyable, and exciting!

Try adding any of the healthy fats listed in the following chart to your raw fresh vegetable juices. Certain nutrients, such as vitamins A, E, D, and K, and some essential minerals such as magnesium and zinc, are fat soluble. Therefore, adding a healthy fat to your juice provides a carrier for optimal absorption and transport. You are what you absorb!

Follow the basic chart. The combinations are endless. You're limited only by your imagination.

Start with your high-water-content fruits or vegetables as your Base 1 or Base 2, then add either your favorite citrus or other fruits, leafy greens, roots, herbs, and healthy fats. Go ahead—go wild!

Note: Some combinations don't play well together. Here are those that do:

- Base 1 combines well with greens, roots, herbs, lemon/lime, healthy fats, and add-ins.
- Base 1 (except tomato) combines well with citrus, greens, herbs, healthy fats, and add-ins.
- Base 1 (except tomato) combines well with roots, greens, herbs, lemon/lime, healthy fats, and add-ins.
- Base 1 (except tomato) combines well with fruit, greens, herbs, lemon/lime, healthy fats, and add-ins.
- Base 2 combines well with greens, citrus, herbs, and add-ins.

Base 1: Choose one or two or a combination of all three.	Celery stalks Cucumbers Tomatoes
Base 2: Choose one.	Watermelon Honeydew Cantaloupe Pineapple
Citrus: Choose one.	Lemons Limes Oranges Tangelos Grapefruit
Greens: Choose one to two handfuls or a combination thereof.	Spinach Kale Chard Arugula Lettuce Leeks Collards Dandelion greens Green onion Bell pepper Romaine Or other leafy greens
Roots and Extras: Choose one or a combination thereof.	Carrots Beets Parsnips Turmeric Ginger Garlic Daikon Radishes Fennel

Herbs: Choose one or any combination thereof.	Cilantro Parsley Thyme Oregano Rosemary Tarragon Chives Sage Dill Mint Basil
Fruit or Berry: Choose 1	Apple Pear Grapes Blueberries
Healthy Fats: Choose one and blend in after juicing.	1 teaspoon to 1 tablespoon coconut oil 1 teaspoon to 1 tablespoon flax oil 1 teaspoon to 1 tablespoon avocado oil 1 teaspoon to 1 tablespoon flax/chia seeds ¼ to ½ avocado 1 tablespoon nut butter ¼ cup soaked or sprouted nuts
Great Add-Ins (optional)	Dash cinnamon 1 teaspoon to 1 tablespoon apple cider vinegar 1 teaspoon to 1 tablespoon coconut cider vinegar Pinch sea salt Dash cayenne

Welcome to The Green Aisle's Juice Bar: Recipes

Morning Juice Bar

Fresca   60
Wake-Up Call   60
Waldorf   60
Superfood Tea   60
Grapefruit Fizz   61

Fresca

Yield 1 serving, 8 ounces

Ingredients
1 large cucumber
2 cups spinach
2 cups grapes
½ cup mineral water

Directions
Juice all ingredients and enjoy.

Wake-Up Call

Yield 1 serving, 8 ounces

Ingredients
18 mint leaves, stem attached
2 lemons, peeled
¼ cup sparkling water
2 teaspoons maple syrup

Directions
Juice mint and lemon while pouring the sparkling water into the juicer to help extract the juice from the mint leaves. Pour juice into a shaker bottle, add maple syrup; shake vigorously, pour over ice.

Waldorf

Yield 1 serving, 8 ounces

Ingredients
¼ cup walnuts, presoak
½ cup spring water
2 celery stalks
1 cups red grapes

Directions
Soak walnuts in enough water to cover them for up to 4 hours; drain and rinse. Combine all ingredients, along with ½ cup spring water, inside your juicer, and let the juicing begin.

Superfood Tea

Yield 1 serving, 8 ounces

Ingredients
16 oz. water
½ cup carrot, grated
½ cup daikon or parsnips, grated
2-inch piece kombu, broken into pieces
1 tsp. coconut aminos

Directions
Bring water to boil, add carrot, daikon or parsnips, and kombu. Reduce heat, simmer for 3 to 5 minutes. Add coconut aminos and stir. Drink while hot, munchin' on veggies!

Grapefruit Fizz

Yield 1 serving, 8 ounces

Ingredients
Sea salt (optional to rim glass)
4 ice cubes
1 grapefruit, yields approx. ⅔ cup
⅓ cup Q Club Soda

Directions
Wet the rim of your glass and dip onto sea salt, pour in ice cubes; set glass aside. Juice grapefruit with citrus juicer. Using your juicer may yield pulp. Pour juice and Q Club Soda into a shaker bottle; vigorously shake and pour over ice and enjoy.

Smoothie Bar

Matcha Madness   65
Libido Enhancer   66
PB&J   66
Cherry Watermelon Sport Sipper   67
Citrus Sunshine Sexy Smoothie   68
Pineapple Upside-Down Cake   69

Matcha Madness

Yield 2 servings, 16 ounces

Ingredients

1 teaspoon matcha powder
½ cup warm water
1 cup almond mylk or preferred mylk
½ banana
1 tablespoon vanilla protein powder
1 cup spinach
1 tablespoon agave
10 ice cubes

Directions

Combine matcha with warm water; whisk well. Combine matcha mixture, along with all other ingredients into a high-speed blender and blend until smooth; top with non-dairy whipped cream or fresh coconut whipped cream found on page 190.

Note:

The crazy matcha green tea leaf is packed with rich chlorophyll and is superior in its effects for blood detoxification and mood enhancement. It is energy-boosting and stress-reducing and combats inflammation, oxidation, and aging. It supports mind clarity and alertness and boosts immunity. It has powerful anticarcinogenic properties and high fiber content and contains more antioxidants than a cup of green tea or goji berries. It may also lower cholesterol and lower blood pressure. If that isn't enough, try drinking this Matcha Madness before a workout and melt 25 percent more of that stubborn body fat. You can find this recipe and more like it in *The Green Aisle's Healthy Smoothies and Slushies.*

Be sure to choose a protein such as pea protein, brown rice protein, or sprouted nuts, seeds, beans, or grains. Avoid protein powder that contains whey, soy, dairy, or casein for cleansing purposes.

Libido Enhancer

Yield 2 servings, 16 ounces

Ingredients

16 ounces almond mylk or preferred mylk
1 tablespoon maca root powder
1 teaspoon moringa leaf powder
1 tablespoon chia seeds
3 tablespoons vanilla protein powder (see note on page 65)

Directions

Blend all ingredients in a high-speed blender and blend until smooth.

PB&J

Yield 2 servings, 16 ounces

Ingredients

16 ounces almond mylk or preferred mylk
2½ cups mixed berries: strawberry, blackberry, raspberry
1 banana
2 tablespoons peanut butter

Directions

Blend all ingredients in a high-speed blender and blend until smooth.

Cherry Watermelon Sport Sipper

Yield 1 serving, 8 ounces

Ingredients
3 cups watermelon chunks, frozen
1 cup cherries, pitted
1 cup coconut water

Directions
Thaw watermelon chunks just a bit to allow the blades to blend smoothly. Frozen pitted cherries work great; defrost before blending.

Blend all ingredients in a high-speed blender and blend until smooth.

Citrus Sunshine Sexy Smoothie

Yield 4 servings, 32 ounces

Ingredients
3 oranges, juiced
1 lemon, juiced
1 cups almond mylk
1 banana
⅛ teaspoon ashwaganda powder
¼ teaspoon matcha green tea powder
1½ teaspoons vanilla protein powder (see note on page 65)
2 cups frozen fruit blend: peaches, mango pineapple, strawberry
4–6 ice cubes
Garnish with cinnamon

Directions
Juice orange and lemon with a citrus juicer, pour into a high-speed blender with all other ingredients, and blend until creamy. Top with a dash of cinnamon. Portion your Citrus Sunshine Sexy Smoothie in 8-ounce mason jars, secure lids, and refrigerate for the next day.

Note:
This recipe was inspired by Harley Harris. He would remind you to use a citrus juicer to omit the pulp from the oranges and lemon!

Pineapple Upside-Down Cake

Yield 2 servings, 16 ounces

Ingredients
1 orange, juiced, approx. ½ cup
½ cup coconut mylk
½ banana
1 cup pineapple chunks, frozen
6 large mint leaves

Directions
Juice orange with a citrus juicer, pour into a high-speed blender with all other ingredients, and blend until creamy.

Detox Juice Bar

Oxidative Stress Reliever

Oxidative Stress Reliever

Yield 1 serving 8 ounces

Ingredients
1 cup spinach
1 cup parsley
2 celery stalks
1 carrot

Directions
Juice all ingredients and enjoy.

Celery Stick

Yield 1 serving 8 ounces

Ingredients
4 celery stalks
½ apple
¼ lemon, peeled

Directions
Juice all ingredients and enjoy.

Licorice Stick

Yield 2 servings, 16 ounces

Ingredients
1 small or medium fennel bulb
   with fronds
½ green apple
¾ English cucumber

Directions
Juice all ingredients and enjoy.

Immunity Juice Elixir

Yield 1 serving, 8 ounces

1 green bell pepper
3 celery stalks
1 red jalapeño or red Fresno chile
2 green onions
1 handful cilantro
1 lemon, peeled

Directions
Juice all ingredients and enjoy.

Note:
Who would have thought bell peppers contain more vitamin C than an orange? This amazing garden veggie can boost the immune system. This recipe combines it with celery, a base for many juices due to its high-water content, one of the most hydrating and alkalizing vegetables the body needs to create a perfect pH harmony, along with lemon to help relieve coughs and allergies. You're on the right track with this Immunity Juice Elixir!

Grass Roots

Monster Mash

Yield 2 servings, 16 ounces

Ingredients
1 cucumber
½-inch ginger root
1 apple, cored
6 large kale leaves
1 lemon peeled

Directions
Juice all ingredients and enjoy.

Grass Roots

Yield 2 servings, 16 ounces

Ingredients
½ cup wheatgrass blades, washed
   (homemade, page 89)
1 smidgeon/half-pinch ginger root
1 large beetroot

Directions
Juice all ingredients and enjoy.

Note:
Pictured on the previous page and
inspired by Bebe L. Savage, Holistic
Health Coach.

Pickle Juice

Yield 2 servings, 16 ounces

Ingredients
1 English cucumber
1 cup fresh dill, roughly chopped
1 lemon, peeled
Garnish with sea salt

Directions
Juice all ingredients. Slightly wet
the rim of your glass, dip it over sea
salt, pour in the pickle juice, and
enjoy!

Kingpin

Yield 2 servings, 16 ounces

Ingredients
1 English cucumber
1 red bell pepper
½ lemon, peeled
Large sprig parsley
Generous dash cayenne

Directions
Juice all ingredients and enjoy.
Pour into serving glass and garnish
with cayenne.

Cabbage Patch

Cabbage Patch

Yield 1 serving, 8 ounces

Ingredients
1 English cucumber
¾ cup red cabbage, chopped
1 kale leaf

Directions
Juice all ingredients and enjoy. Drink immediately.
Taste may change after oxidation and refrigeration.

Mint Refresher

Yield 1 ½ servings, 12 ounces

Ingredients
1 cucumber
1 large pear
6 large mint leaves
1 lime, peeled

Directions
Juice all ingredients and enjoy.

Green Gator Aide

Yield 4 servings, 32 ounces

Ingredients
3 celery stalks
1 cucumber
3 lemons, with rind
1 apple
¼–½ inch turmeric root

Directions
Juice all ingredients and portion juice in 8-ounce mason jars, secure lid, and refrigerate. Drink throughout the day.

Dirt and Radish Crunch

Yield 1½ servings, 12 ounces

Ingredients
2 tomatoes
2 red chard leaves, stems included
1 lemon, peeled partially
1 yellow bell pepper
2 celery stalks
2 radishes (not juiced)
Garnish with pinch of sea salt and
    cayenne pepper

Directions
Juice all ingredients, except radishes and garnish. Fill glass and top with garnish. Drink while munching on radishes.

Cider Snap Shot

Yield 1 serving, 8 ounces

Ingredients
1 English cucumber
1 apple
1 kale leaf
½ lemon, peeled
Sliver ginger
½ teaspoon coconut cider vinegar
    or apple cider vinegar
Dash Chinese 5-spice powder

Directions
Juice all ingredients, except cider vinegar and Chinese 5-spice powder. Pour juice into a shaker bottle, add cider vinegar and Chinese 5-spice powder; vigorously shake and enjoy.

Celery Mint Cleanser

Yield 1 serving, 8 ounces

Ingredients
2 celery stalks
1 green apple
10 mint leaves, stems attached

Directions
Juice all ingredients and enjoy.

El Conquistador

Yield 2 servings, 16 ounces

Ingredients
1 red bell pepper
3 celery stalks
3–4 vine-ripened tomatoes
1 lemon, peeled
3 small garlic cloves
4 romaine leaves
Small handful cilantro
1 small carrot
Garnish with a dash of sea salt and
    cayenne

Directions
Juice all ingredients and garnish
with sea salt and cayenne.

Chili Texan V-8 Juice

Yield 2 servings, 16 ounces

Ingredients
2 garlic cloves
½ cup cilantro
1 green bell pepper
½ lime, skin removed
2 cups baby kale
1 green onion
4 tomatoes
2 carrots
Garnish with a dash of chili powder
    and sea salt

Directions
Juice all ingredients and garnish
with chili powder and sea salt. You
may even opt to roll the rim of the
glass with a lime wedge and dip the
edges in the chili powder and sea
salt mixture; great for parties.

Bottoms Up

Flu Shot

Yield 1 serving, 4 ounces

Ingredients
1 beet, washed thoroughly
1 lemon, peeled
2 garlic cloves

Directions
Juice all ingredients and drink immediately.

Note:
Beets satiate sweet cravings and cleanse the blood and colon. They contain calcium, iron, magnesium, phosphorous, folic acid (which is important for the growth of new cells), niacin, and vitamins C and A. As a big added bonus, they can prevent several kinds of cancers and heart issues. Allicin found in raw fresh garlic contains potent medicinal properties to help combat your seasonal cold/flu. Pictured on the next page.

Sweet and Spicy

Yield 1 serving, 4 ounces

Ingredients
1 cup fresh pineapple, peel removed, core intact
1 inch ginger root

Directions
Juice all ingredients and drink immediately.

Ginger Shot

Yield 1 serving, 2 ounces

Ingredients
2 tablespoon lemon, juiced
1 tablespoon Ginger People Ginger Juice
Garnish with a dash of cayenne

Directions
Squeeze lemon into shot glass, top with ginger juice and a dash of cayenne, and drink immediately.

Note:
Ginger People Ginger Juice is a time-saver. It is premade for ease of use and can be found in most health food supermarkets.

Flu Shot

Growing Wheatgrass—Made Simple

Ingredients
1 cup of wheatgrass seeds
10-by-20-inch tray with small multiple drain holes with lid or cover
Organic soil
Azomite

Directions

Pre-sprout
Rinse wheatgrass seeds; drain. Soak the seeds immersed in water for about 8–10 hours. Next, drain, and resoak the wheatgrass seeds as above for an additional 8–10 hours; drain.

Preparing the Tray
Fill the tray with organic soil and moisten lightly with a water spray bottle. Place the tray on top of the lid or cover to catch debris and drainage.

Lay the seeds evenly and densely on the dampened soil. Gently press the seeds into the soil. Sprinkle a thin layer of Azomite (a brand of rock-dust powder) over the top of the seeds and cover with a couple dampened paper towels. Situate your tray in indirect sunlight, inside your house near a window and with proper ventilation. Wheatgrass does not like hot direct sunlight.

Watering
Keep seeds moist. If the soil gets dry, the young shoots may die off before they sprout. Continue to re-dampen paper towels and cover seeds, checking periodically. When the shoots start to sprout, in approximately 3 days, remove the paper towels and reduce watering to once a day. Always ensure that the water is just enough to keep the soil damp to the roots. Avoid overwatering.

After sprouting, remove the paper towels; continue to spray shoots daily with water. When the wheatgrass grows to approximately 6 inches, about day 9 or 10, it is ready for juicing. Use scissors and cut the wheatgrass just above the roots. Cut just prior to juicing to ensure freshness. Always rinse and/or soak the wheatgrass to remove any dirt or debris before juicing. Place in a hand manual wheatgrass juicer or juicer specifically designed to extract this amazingly powerful detoxifier. I used the Hurricane Stainless Steel Manual Wheatgrass Juicer.

Wheatgrass Shot

Yield 1 serving, 4 ounces

Ingredients
5 cups wheatgrass blades, washed (page 89)
¼ cups water
1 orange, wedge (optional)

Directions
Wash wheatgrass thoroughly, and juice blades of grass in your manual wheatgrass juicer. Using a manual wheatgrass juicer will yield more juice per ounce and water is not required. Pour into a shot glass, drink immediately, and enjoy your orange wedge as a chaser.

Or you may opt to juice wheatgrass in your fruit and vegetable juicer, alternately pouring a bit of water at a time to help extract the juice from your grass. Pour into a shot glass, drink immediately, and enjoy your orange wedge as a chaser.

Notes:
Wheatgrass contains up to 70 percent chlorophyll (a superfood and blood purifier). It provides amino acids and essential vitamins and minerals, including vitamin A, C, E, phosphorus, iron, calcium, magnesium, and potassium. It is highly alkaline, which has multiple healing properties and protects against: acne, premature aging, anemia,

arthritis, asthma, bladder disorders, blood pressure (high or low), bone disorders, bronchitis, cancer, circulatory weakness, colitis, constipation, diabetes, eye disorders, fatigue, hay fever, hair loss, heart disease, hypoglycemia, impotence, infection, kidney disorders, liver disorders, lung disorders, nervous disorders, skin disorders, and ulcers.

Wheatgrass supports weight loss, detoxifies and rebuilds the bloodstream, prevents tooth decay and strengthens gums, improves glucose and lipid levels, and helps purify the liver and cleanse drug deposits from the body.

To yield as much wheatgrass juice as possible, after the first juice cycle, you may opt to run the pulp and wheatgrass juice through your juicer two to three times to make sure you're getting optimal extraction.

Iron-rich produce (wheatgrass) followed by vitamin C (orange) increases the body's ability to absorb iron into your red blood cells. This allows the body to use the mineral iron to create hemoglobin (protein molecule), which carries oxygen throughout the body for energy.

Happy Hour Juice Bar

Sour Apple Patch

Sour Apple Patch Juice

Yield 2 servings, 16 ounces

Ingredients
4 green apples, juiced
2 lemons, juiced
1 cup mineral water

Directions
Juice apple and lemon (use a citrus juice to omit pulp), combine it with mineral water, and blend in a high-speed blender for a few seconds or pour into a shaker bottle and shake vigorously; pour over ice and consume.

Jolly Green Giant

Yield 1½ servings, 12 ounces

Ingredients
2 green apples
3 celery stalks
½ lemon, peeled
1 teaspoon apple cider vinegar or coconut cider vinegar
Dash cayenne

Directions
Juice apple, celery, and lemon. Pour into a shaker bottle and add cider vinegar and cayenne. Shake vigorously; drink immediately.

Bayou Juice

Yield 2 servings, 16 ounces

Ingredients
5 kale leaves
½ cucumber
Handful spinach
½ celery stalk
1 orange, peeled
½ apple
Sliver ginger
1 lemon, wedge

Directions
Juice all ingredients and enjoy.

Note:

This concoction contains vitamins A, K, C, and B6, manganese, calcium, copper, potassium, magnesium, B1, B2, B3, iron, and phosphorus. Can't get your kids to eat greens? Just tell them it's Shrek's favorite swampy drink: Bayou Juice!

Watermelon Candy Cane

Yield 4 servings, 32 ounces

Ingredients
Sugar baby watermelon, rind intact or discarded
8 large peppermint leaves

Directions
Cut watermelon to fit juicer. Let the juicing begin by adding mint leaves intermittently while juicing the watermelon. Pour over ice and garnish with fresh mint sprigs. Great for a summer pool party. Portion juice in 8-ounce mason jars, secure lid, and refrigerate. Drink throughout the day.

Notes:
Watermelons contain powerful antioxidants called lycopene that neutralize free radicals and reduce the severity of asthma, prostate and colon cancer, heart disease, and rheumatoid arthritis. Watermelon contains more lycopene than any other fruit or vegetable. Plus, vitamin B—energy production; B_6 and B_1, magnesium, potassium, manganese, vitamin C and A. And watermelon *rind* contains up to 95 percent of the nutrient and is edible.

Try freezing watermelon juice for a nice and refreshing popsicle, or juice it along with a little citrus juice for a great grab-and-go hydrating, cooling, and energizing drink for the hot summer.

Bunny Juice

Bunny Juice

Yield 1 serving, 8 ounces

Ingredients
8 carrots
½ lemons, peeled
1 sliver ginger

Directions
Juice all ingredients and enjoy.

Woo Woo

Yield 1 serving, 8 ounces

Ingredients
1 nectarine or peach, pit removed
1 cup cranberries
¼ cup water or mineral water

Directions
Juice all ingredients; pour over ice
and enjoy.

Note:
Use prefrozen cranberries; defrost
on countertop to room temperature
before juicing. Juicing whole raw
cranberries may destroy your juicer.

Peppered Pineapple

Yield 1 serving, 8 ounces

Ingredients
3 cups fresh pineapple, peel removed,
   core intact
3 cups arugula

Directions
Juice all ingredients and enjoy.

Brain Teaser

Yield 2 servings, 16 ounces

Ingredients
1 pear
1 apple
4 celery stalks
1 lemon, peeled
1 cup arugula

Directions
Juice all ingredients and enjoy.

Note:
This recipe was inspired by Bebe
Savage, Certified Health Coach.

Snappy Beet

Pumpkin Patch

Yield 1½ servings, 12 ounces

Ingredients

1 sugar pie pumpkin, peeled, seeded, diced
2 small apples
1 pear
¼ lemon, peeled
Pinch ginger root
1–2 tablespoons water
¼ teaspoon pumpkin pie spice
¼ teaspoon cinnamon

Directions

Combine pumpkin, apple, pear, lemon, ginger, and water inside your juicer, and let the juicing begin. Pour juice into a shaker bottle, add pumpkin pie spice and cinnamon; shake and enjoy.

Snappy Beet

Yield 1 serving, 8 ounces

Ingredients

1 beet, thoroughly washed
1 small apple
½ inch ginger root
4 mint leaves

Directions

Juice all ingredients and enjoy.

Hawaii Five-O

Yield 1 serving, 8–10 ounces

Ingredients
2 cups fresh pineapple, peel removed, core intact
1 cup wheatgrass, grass blades

Directions
Juice all ingredients and enjoy.

Cutie Twist

Yield 1½ servings, 12 ounces

Ingredients
1 cucumber
3 tangerines, peeled
1 cup baby kale leaves

Directions
Juice all ingredients and enjoy.

Slingshot Turbo Malibu

Yield 1 serving, 8 ounces

Ingredients

2 cups fresh pineapple, peel removed, core intact
1 fresh Thai coconut; ½ cup coconut water and all coconut meat*
1 lime, wedge (optional)

Directions

Slice and dice fresh pineapple to fit into juicer; set aside. Intermittently juice pineapple, along with ½ cup coconut water and coconut meat. Pour over ice, slide lime over the rim of your glass and squeeze a bit of lime juice over the top of your juice, and enjoy. Store remaining coconut water in a mason jar and refrigerate; add to any smoothie or juice recipe.

Notes:

Coconut water has 5 essential electrolytes: sodium; 600 milligrams of potassium; phosphorus; 60 milligrams of magnesium, and 2 grams of protein. It's a superfood that contains electrolytes identical to those of human blood. Coconut water (straight from the coconut, not processed) is a great source of ultimate hydration, and contains a multitude of minerals, antioxidants, enzymes, and vitamins, and maintains a proper pH balance.

As we discussed in *The Green Aisle's Healthy Smoothies and Slushies*, it's not a problem if you can't find any fresh coconuts. Nothing will taste as good as using a fresh coconut, but there are alternatives.

Exotic Superfood Young Thai 100 percent raw coconut meat can be purchased in the frozen section of your local health food supermarket or online. Allow coconut meat to thaw on counter to room temperature before use. Bottled coconut water can also be substituted; just be sure there are no added sugars or preservatives.

Want a quick way to open your coconut in just seconds? I love my Coco-Jack! One investment that keeps on giving. Just go to coco-jack.com to place your order.

Tart Cherry Juice

Last Call

Turmeric Latte

Yield 1½ servings, 12 ounces

Ingredients

1½ cups coconut mylk
1 cinnamon stick
1-inch piece fresh turmeric root, chopped
1-inch piece fresh ginger root, chopped

Directions

Combine all ingredients in a small saucepan and cook on low for 20 minutes. Strain into a mug and sip before bed.

Notes:

Turmeric has been used in India for more than 2,500 years for its medicinal health benefits. Cancer and other chronic diseases are less often seen in India versus the Western countries, in part because of use of this powerful root. It is also a natural liver detoxifier, prevents and stops the growth of prostate cancer, removes amyloid plaque in the brain (which causes Alzheimer's disease), is an anti-inflammatory that helps alleviate arthritis, and slows the progression of multiple sclerosis.

Tart Cherry Juice

Yield 1 serving, 8 ounces

Ingredients
2 tablespoons tart cherry juice concentrate
8 ounces water

Directions
Mix ingredients in a shaker bottle, shake vigorously, and drink before bed.

Notes:
Tart cherry juice can be found at your local health food supermarkets or online. There are many brands. Choose one that is organic with no added sugars. The ingredients should say only tart cherry juice and/or tart cherry juice concentrate. Tart cherry juice contains magnesium to calm the nerves and send a message to your brain to "shut down" so you can fall asleep with ease. Magnesium also acts as an osmotic laxative to relax bowels, soften stools, and allow poo to pass easily.

Foods highest in magnesium: swiss chard, spinach, dark cocoa powder, almonds.

Sad Fact: Did you know the process of refining grains removes 80 to 97 percent of the magnesium found in whole grains?

Chia Gel

Yield 1 serving, 4 ounces

Ingredients
½ cup water, juice blend, or coconut water
2 tablespoons chia seeds

Directions
Combine ingredients in a small glass, stir, and allow to set for approximately 20 minutes. This allows the seeds to soak up and absorb the liquid from your water, juice blend, or coconut water rather than bodily fluids. Drink and enjoy.

Notes:
Chia seeds are an ancient Mesoamerican superfood, high in omega-3 fatty acids, vitamins, minerals, and fiber. Two tablespoons of chia have more omega-3 fatty acids than two servings of salmon, without the risk of consuming heavy metals, plus they lubricate the colon to aid in bowel regularity and healthy stools.

Blood Orange Aloe Vera

Yield 1 serving, 4 ounces

Ingredients
1 lemon, juiced
1 blood orange, juiced
2 tablespoons aloe vera juice

Directions
Juice lemon and blood orange with your citrus juicer into a small glass; add aloe vera juice and stir. Drink and enjoy.

Notes:
Egyptians called aloe the Plant of Immortality for its health, beauty, and medicinal skin care properties. Centuries later, aloe is still being used for its many health benefits, from external to internal. Just cut the aloe plant and gently apply the gel to a sunburn topically, as the cleansing and antiseptic properties will heal and soothe. Aloe contains 75 active properties including enzymes, minerals, salicylic acids, amino acids, vitamins A, C, E, and B_{12}, and so much more. It is used as a natural remedy for constipation, reduces inflammation, detoxifies the body, supports the immune system, and aids in digestive issues.

Aloe vera juice can be found at your local health food market; purchase liquid, not gel. Be sure it is at least 99 percent pure aloe vera without added sugars or flavor enhancers.

Important: If you take warfarin or are on any other prescribed medications or have a medical condition, please consult with your doctor before taking aloe. Do not consume aloe in large doses or over a prolonged period of time as it will cause painful abdominal cramping and diarrhea. It may also lower blood sugar levels.

Fizzy Lime Drop

Yield 1 serving, 8 ounces

Ingredients
½ cup coconut water kefir
½ cup coconut water
1 lime, juiced
Sliver ginger root
1 tablespoon agave (optional)

Directions
Blend all ingredients on high for 40 seconds or until smooth. If you are new to coconut water kefir, you may opt to use ¼ cup coconut water kefir and ¾ cup of coconut water until you're used to the flavor.

Notes:
Kefir means "feel good" in Turkish. It's an enzyme-rich food filled with beneficial microorganisms to balance your inner ecosystem, creating happy microflora in your gut. Coconut water kefir has 100 billion probiotic CFUs per one tablespoon. It's a superfood that contains electrolytes identical to those of human blood. It's the best in hydration; has tons of minerals, antioxidants, enzymes, and vitamins; maintains a proper pH; and is one of the best probiotics on the market.

Coconut water kefir can be found at your local health food supermarket or can be made at home. See Rachel Feldman's Homemade Coconut Water Kefir recipe found on page 166.

The Fizzy Lime Drop recipe first appeared in *The Green Aisle's Healthy Smoothies and Slushies*. Don't forget to check it out!

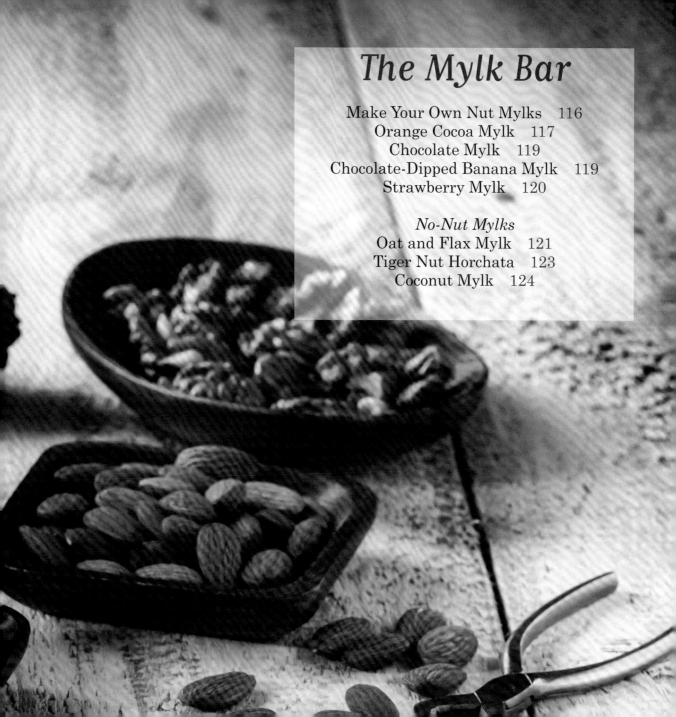

The Mylk Bar

Make Your Own Nut Mylks

Yield 4 servings, 32 ounces

Ingredients
1 cup almonds or other preferred nut
2 dates, pitted
4 cups water

Directions
Combine all ingredients in a bowl, cover with cheesecloth or a paper towel, and allow to soak for 8 to 12 hours. Juice all ingredients, along with water, pour into a glass container; seal and refrigerate. Use as desired for up to 3 days; shake before each use.

Notes:
To yield as much mylk as possible, after the first juice cycle, you may opt to run the pulp and nut mylk through your juicer two to three times to make sure you're getting optimal extraction; then pour, seal, and store in refrigerator.

Orange Cocoa Mylk

Yield 2 servings, 16 ounces

Ingredients
1 cup almond or other preferred nut mylk
2 oranges, juiced, approx. 1 cup
2 tablespoons cocoa powder

Directions
Juice orange with a citrus juicer to avoid pulp.
Combine all ingredients in a high-speed blender
and blend until creamy.

Note:
Prefer dark chocolate? Use cacao powder instead.

Chocolate Mylk

Yield 1 serving, 8 ounces

Ingredients
2 cups nut mylk or other preferred mylk
2 tablespoons cacao powder
2 tablespoons maple syrup
Garnish with cinnamon or cayenne pepper (optional)

Directions
Combine all ingredients in a high-speed blender and blend until smooth; pour into a glass and top with your favorite garnish.

Chocolate-Dipped Banana Mylk

Yield 1½ servings, 12 ounces

Ingredients
12 ounces nut mylk or other preferred mylk
3 tablespoons cacao powder
2–3 tablespoons maple syrup
1 banana
Garnish with cinnamon or cayenne pepper (optional)

Directions
Combine all ingredients in a high-speed blender and blend until smooth; pour into a glass and top with your favorite garnish.

Strawberry Mylk

Yield 4 servings, 32 ounces

Ingredients
1 cup almonds
2 cups strawberries
4 dates, pitted
4 cups water

Directions
Combine all ingredients in a large bowl, cover with cheesecloth or a paper towel, and allow to soak for 8 to 12 hours. Juice all soaked ingredients, along with water, pour into a glass container; seal and refrigerate. Use as desired for up to 3 days; shake before each use.

Note:
To yield as much flavor as possible, after the first juice cycle, you may opt to run the pulp and strawberry mylk through your juicer two to three times to make sure you're getting optimal extraction; then pour, seal, and store in refrigerator

Oat and Flax Mylk

Yield 4 servings, 32 ounces

Oat mylk is a great alternative for those who have nut, soy, or dairy allergies. It is high in fiber, calcium, protein, and some B vitamins. Steel-cut oats are more nutritious than rolled as they have not been stripped of the bran and germ. Add a bit of flax to your oat mylk for beneficial Omega-3 fatty acids.

Ingredients
4 cups water
1 cup steel-cut oats
2 tablespoon flaxseeds (optional)
2 dates, pitted (optional)

Directions
Combine all ingredients in a bowl, cover with cheesecloth or a paper towel, and allow to soak overnight. Blend in a high-speed blender until creamy; strain in a mylk nut bag or through cheesecloth. Pour into a glass container; seal and refrigerate. Use as desired for up to 3 days; shake before each use.

Tiger Nut Horchata

Yield 4 servings, 32 ounces

Ingredients
1 cup tiger nuts (tubers)
4 cups water
½ tsp. alcohol-free vanilla extract or vanilla powder
¼ tsp. cinnamon

Directions
Combine tiger nuts with a generous amount of warm water, cover with cheesecloth or a paper towel, and allow to soak overnight 12 – 24 hours; drain. Combine water, tiger nuts, vanilla, and cinnamon in a high-speed blender and blend until creamy. Pour into a glass container; seal and refrigerate. Use as desired for up to 3 days; shake before each use.

Note:
The term *tiger nut* is a bit deceiving. They're not nuts at all; they are sweet nutrient-dense tubers, small root vegetables that our earliest human ancestors consumed for fuel. A tiger nut is a whole food, a resistant starch, and a prebiotic fiber that resists human digestion and becomes fuel for our probiotic bacteria. A healthy gut makes a happy human. You can eat them raw, soaked, or turned into horchata (tiger nut mylk). If you decide to eat them raw or soaked, be sure to chew them thoroughly as they're fibrous; then you'll start to experience their sweet nutty flavor.

Coconut Mylk

Yield 4 servings, 32 ounces

Ingredients
1 young Thai coconut

Directions
Open the young Thai coconut and pour the coconut water into a bowl. Scoop out all of the soft coconut meat and place it in the bowl with the coconut water.

Juice all the coconut meat and coconut water, pour into a glass container; seal and refrigerate. Use as desired for up to 3 days; shake before each use.

For a thinner mylk, add ¼ cup water at a time until you reach desired consistency.

Notes:
One fresh young Thai coconut yields approximately 1½ cups coconut water and ½ cup coconut meat; use everything you can get out of the coconut.

Coconuts get a bad rap for their saturated fat, but healthy fats are essential to dietary needs, unlike trans fats, which are contained in dairy and animal fats. Coconuts can have many useful benefits, aiding in immune function, reduction of heart disease, and weight loss. Weight loss—really? Yes. Persons who include some healthy fats in their diet curb appetite, satiate sugar cravings, stay full longer, increase metabolism, and tend to stay thin. Coconut mylk has antibacterial and antiviral properties, which aid in the fight against viruses and bacteria.

To yield as much coconut mylk as possible, after the first juice cycle, you may opt to run the pulp and coconut mylk through your juicer two to three times to make sure you're getting optimal extraction; then pour, seal, and store in refrigerator.

Want a quick way to open your coconut in just seconds? I love my Coco-Jack! It's one investment that keeps on giving. Just go to coco-jack.com to place your order.

Breakfast Bar

Simple Cereal Berry Bowl

Yield 1 serving

Ingredients
½ cup strawberries
½ cup blueberries
¼ cup raw pecans
1–2 cups almond or other preferred nut mylk

Directions
Combine all ingredients in a bowl and enjoy!

Note:
Simple cereal berry bowls make breakfast a snap. Opt for fresh, in-season fruits. Try diced apple with pecans, sliced banana with almonds and cinnamon, or fresh figs and pistachios with a dash of cardamom.

Snack Bar

Supercharge Your Body with Raw Snacks!

Or try these . . .

- 2 celery stalks filled with 1 tablespoon almond butter + 3 dried cranberries for each stalk
- 1–2 Perfect Pickles found on page 140
- Small handful tiger nuts (tubers); chew thoroughly
- 1 small apple and ½ cup raisins
- 1 cup preferred nut mylk and 1 dried fig
- Chayote with a bit of lemon and sea salt

- ½ avocado with a pinch of sea salt, turmeric, coriander, and cayenne
- 2 prunes or dried apricots
- Your favorite plant-based protein powder with 8 oz. water
- ¼ cup nuts of your choice, soaked or sprouted
- 1 grapefruit
- Handful of blueberries
- Handful of cherries
- Dragon fruit

Mama's Hummus

Yield 6 servings

2 small cloves garlic
1 can of organic chickpeas, washed and rinsed
½ cup of tahini
1 lemon, juiced
½ cup of water, scant
Salt to taste

Combine all ingredients in a food processor and blend until desired consistency. Add a bit more water if the mixture feels too pasty. Serve with dipping vegetables: carrots, celery, bell pepper, cucumber, or any other favorite vegetable.

This recipe was inspired by Rania Chami, Holistic Health and Wellness Coach.

Beetroot Hummus

Yield 4 servings

Ingredients
½ cup cashews, soaked for 2 hours and drained
1 garlic clove, sliced
1 small beet, shredded, approx. ½ cup
1½ tablespoons lemon, juiced
3 tablespoons water
¼ teaspoon sea salt

Directions
Combine all ingredients in a food processor and blend until desired consistency. Serve with dipping vegetables: carrots, celery, bell pepper, cucumber, or any other favorite vegetable.

Cashew Cream Caprese Triple-Decker

Yield 12 ounces cashew cream

Ingredients for cashew cream
2 cups cashews, soaked for at least 2 hours and drained
3 tablespoons olive oil
4 tablespoons lemon, juiced
1 teaspoon maple syrup
3 cloves garlic
1 tablespoon nutritional yeast
1 teaspoon sea salt
4 tablespoons water
Pepper to taste

Ingredients for Caprese Triple-Decker
1 large heirloom tomato or 2 small tomatoes, per serving
As many large basil leaves as you desire
A bit of cashew cream

Directions
Combine all ingredients for cashew cream in a high-speed blender; blend until smooth, stopping to scrape sides if necessary. You may opt to use a food processor and blend until desired consistency, but this may result in a gritty consistency. Pour cream into a glass container, seal, and refrigerate until use.

Cut tomato into thin slices, top with a dollop of cashew cream and a basil leaf, and repeat until your Triple-Decker is piled high and enjoy.

Spicy Tomatillo Salsa

Yield 6 servings, 3 cups

Ingredients

1 pound tomatillos, unhusked
2 serrano chiles, stems removed (remove seeds for less heat)
½ yellow onion
4–5 medium garlic cloves
¼–½ bundle cilantro, roughly chopped (use amount you desire)
1 teaspoon sea salt
1 lime, juiced, approx. 2 tablespoons
Pepper to taste

Directions

Broil tomatillos and serrano chiles on a sheet pan until the skin starts to char and split, approximately 15 to 20 minutes. Allow to cool and remove skins and stems; discard. Combine all ingredients in a food processor and puree until desired consistency.

Cover and refrigerate for a few hours for flavors to infuse. One serving size is ½ cup salsa; best served with a variety of cut vegetables: carrots, celery, bell pepper, cucumber, or any other favorite vegetable. Also great with Beanito chips, chips made from beans, not corn.

The Perfect Pickle

Yield 6–7 servings

Ingredients

6–7 Persian or mini cucumbers
16 ounces filtered water, amount may vary, approx 2 cups
2 teaspoons pickling seasoning (I recommend Spicely Organics)
1 tablespoon sea salt
32-ounce mason jar
1 large kale or grape leaf
Garnish Ideas: garlic clove, red pepper flakes, cumin, bay leaf, onion

Directions

Squeeze in as many cucumbers you can fit into the mason jar until they are hugging tightly, add cold water to cover pickles and place in the refrigerator to revive and perk up cucumbers a bit. Add seasoning and salt and any other garnish ideas to make it your own unique blend; seal lid and shake vigorously. Remove the lid and gently place kale or grape leaf over the top; press down. Cover mason jar with cheesecloth or a napkin to keep your pickles clean. Allow to sit on your countertop for 3 to 7 days. When you see bubbles start to form on the top of the pickles, the fermentation is starting.

Give those lil pups a taste on day 3, day 4, and so on, until you have created the ideal taste and crunch; then refrigerate.

Asparagus Soup

Liquid Lunch Bar

Macrobiotic Healing Soup

Yield 2 servings, 16 ounces

Ingredients
2-inch strip of kombu, broken into pieces
⅓ of a celery bunch, inner soft pieces chopped
4 cups water
1 garlic clove, minced
2–4 asparagus spears, fibrous ends removed; discard. Thinly chop spears
¼ tsp. ginger powder or one thin slice of fresh ginger root, minced
4 fresh basil leaves (optional)
10 spinach leaves (optional)
1 teaspoon sea salt
1 tablespoon chickpea miso paste, to be added after simmering

Directions
Place all ingredients into a pot, except miso paste, and bring to a boil. Cover, reduce heat, and simmer for 10 to 15 minutes. Turn off heat. Place miso in a small bowl; add 4 tablespoons of soup broth; whisk until creamy. Pour into soup, stir, and simmer 2 minutes. Add a bit more sea salt if desired. Crushed red pepper flakes are a great add-in too.

Notes:
Kombu's amazing health benefits include essential trace minerals, vitamin B_{12}, and vitamin D. Kombu detoxifies the body by binding to heavy metals and expels toxins from the body, protects against gamma radiation, aids in digestion, improves blood circulation, prevents constipation, balances alkaline and acid in the body, (thus preventing cancer), and aids in a stronger nervous system.

Kombu is a cancer-fighting food. This is an awesome recipe that you can whip together and eat in 15 minutes using just about anything you have left over in your fridge. The options are endless, and you can never go wrong with this healing soup.

Do not boil miso or it will lose its powerful enzymes.

Miso will help to reestablish your intestinal tract and create healthy microflora, creating greater digestion and a healthier pH within the digestive tract. This soup is always healing to the gut when you've bombarded your system with an overload of unhealthy foods and feel bloated.

Asparagus Soup

Yield 2 servings

Ingredients
1 large bundle fresh asparagus, approx. 3 cups spears
½–1 small yellow onion, chopped
1 tablespoon olive oil
2½ cups low-sodium vegetable broth, divided
½ cup cashews, soaked for at least 2 hours or overnight; drain
1 lemon, juiced
salt and pepper, to taste

Directions
Snap the large fibrous ends off the asparagus and discard. Set aside a few spears, if desired, for garnish. Break spears into pieces and sauté with onion in olive oil in a saucepan for approximately 5 minutes.

Add 2 cups vegetable broth and cook until asparagus is slightly tender; approximately 7 minutes. Combine softened cashews, lemon juice, salt and pepper, and ½ cup vegetable broth into a high-speed blender; puree. Combine cooked asparagus, onion, and broth with the cashew cream base; puree until creamy and smooth. Pour into serving bowls and garnish with asparagus spears.

Arugula-Infused Cream of Broccoli Soup

Yield 8 servings

Ingredients

3 medium-sized red potatoes, diced
4 cup broccoli florets
4 ounces vegetable stock
8 ounces water (optional for thinning soup)
4 garlic cloves, smashed
1 yellow onion, sliced
2 tablespoons olive oil
1 teaspoon sea salt, divided
3 cups baby arugula
2 large basil leaves + more for garnish
Garnish Ideas: coconut cream (see note), flaxseeds, chia seeds, pepita (pumpkin seeds), fresh basil, cayenne

Directions

Combine potatoes, broccoli, and vegetable stock in a large saucepan. Bring to a boil, reduce heat to a low boil, cover, and cook for approximately 15 minutes until fork tender.

While the potatoes and broccoli are cooking, sauté garlic and onion in olive oil in a small saucepan, sprinkle ½ teaspoon sea salt over the sauté; cook for approximately 8 minutes or so until onions begin to caramelize. Pour into soup pot when potatoes and broccoli are fork tender; add remaining ½ teaspoon sea salt. Turn off heat and stir in arugula. Pour soup into a high-speed blender for a smooth and creamy consistency; puree. You may need to split the batches for puree. You may opt to use an immersion hand blender directly in the soup pot; this will give your soup more texture. You may opt to add water for a thinner soup at this time for your preferred consistency.

Ladle a bit of soup into your bowl and add your favorite garnish. For one bowl of soup, swirl in 2 to 3 tablespoons coconut cream, ¼ teaspoon flaxseeds, ½ teaspoon chia seeds, a few pepitas, dash of cayenne, and fresh basil.

Notes:

One can organic coconut mylk, in which the only ingredients are coconut, water, and guar gum. Each can contains approximately 1 cup coconut cream. Keep the can in the coldest part of the refrigerator until use. Do not shake can or the cream and liquid will emulsify. You want to keep it separated. After opening, carefully scoop the cream from the top of the can and reserve the liquid for smoothies.

Coconut Curry Sweet Potato Soup

Yield 6 servings

Ingredients

1 yellow onion, diced
6 garlic cloves, smashed
1 tablespoon unrefined coconut oil
2 celery stalks, sliced
4 cups vegetable broth
2 small carrots, diced
2 bay leaves
1 teaspoon sea salt
4 small sweet potatoes, diced
1 tablespoon curry powder
½ teaspoon turmeric
½ teaspoon summer savory powder (optional)
¼ cup coconut cream + a bit more for garnish
Garnish Ideas: drizzle with coconut cream (see note on page 148) or sprinkle with, chopped pumpkin seeds, fresh mint, and basil

Directions

In a large saucepan, sauté onion and garlic in coconut oil until caramelized, stirring occasionally. Add celery and sauté a couple more minutes. Pour vegetable broth into saucepan, along with all other ingredients, except coconut cream. Bring to a boil, reduce heat, simmer for approximately 20 to 30 minutes until sweet potatoes are fork tender. Remove bay leaves; discard. Pour ¼ cup coconut cream over soup and puree with an immersion hand blender directly into the soup pot. Ladle a cup of soup into your bowl, swirl in a bit more coconut cream, and add your favorite garnish, if desired.

Cabbage Lime Fresca

Salad Bar

Orange Poppy Seed Drizzle Salad 153
Curry Parsnip Salad 154
Cabbage Lime Fresca 155
Massaged Kale Salad 157

Orange Poppy Seed Drizzle Salad

Yield 2 servings

2 handfuls baby spinach or preferred bed of greens
½ apple, chopped
⅛–¼ cup dried cranberries
10–15 pecans or walnuts, whole or chopped

3 tablespoons orange balsamic vinegar (I recommend Olive Oil Pantry's)
1 tablespoon olive oil
1 teaspoon poppy seeds
1 tablespoon lemon, juiced
1 teaspoon spicy mustard

Combine the ingredients for salad; toss and divide into two serving bowls. Combine all ingredients for Orange Poppy Seed Drizzle in a small bowl; whisk vigorously and drizzle each bowl with 1 to 2 tablespoons of dressing, per salad. Refrigerate remaining dressing for approximately one or two more salads.

Curry Parsnip Salad

Yield 4 servings

Ingredients
2 parsnips, roughly chopped
3 tablespoons avocado oil
2 tablespoons maple syrup
1½ tablespoons curry powder
Handful dried cranberries
Handful raw cashews, no salt added
1 green onions, minced
2 celery stalks, minced
2 cups baby spinach or mixed greens per serving
Generous pinch sea salt and pepper

Directions
Place parsnips in a food processor, pulsate until the consistency of rice. Combine parsnip rice and all other ingredients, except spinach or mixed greens, in a large bowl; mix well. Place your favorite bed of greens onto a plate and top with parsnip dressing.

Cabbage Lime Fresca

Yield 4–6 servings

Ingredients
½ head cabbage, shredded
½ lime, juiced, approx. 2 tablespoons
2 tablespoons olive oil
½ teaspoon sea salt
½ cup cilantro, chopped
1 green onion, chopped
1 tomato, diced
¼ cucumber, peeled, sliced (optional)
Garnish Ideas: fresh minced dill and/or parsley

Directions
Combine cabbage, lime juice, olive oil, and sea salt in a large bowl; give the cabbage a few hugs, squeezing the mixture together for 2 to 5 minutes. Add cilantro, onion, tomato, and cucumber; toss and refrigerate to chill.

Massaged Kale Salad

Yield 2 servings

Ingredients

6 cups kale leaves, chopped, stems removed and discarded
1–2 garlic cloves, minced (optional)
3 tablespoons lemon, juiced
3 tablespoons olive oil
¼ teaspoon sea salt
Pepper to taste
Garnish Ideas: cranberries, walnuts, sliced almonds, diced apple and chopped walnuts, blueberries and pecans

Directions

Combine kale, garlic, lemon juice, olive oil, sea salt and pepper in a large bowl; give the kale a few hugs, squeezing the mixture together for 2 to 5 minutes until the fibrous kale leaves break down and soften to your liking. Top with your favorite garnish.

Italian Zoodles

Post-Cleanse Bar

Italian Zoodles

Yield 2 servings

Ingredients

2 cups cherry tomatoes
¼ small red onion, chopped, approx. ½ cup
3–4 garlic cloves, minced
2 tablespoons extra virgin olive oil, divided
1 large zucchini, spiralized
½ teaspoon oregano
Pinch sea salt and pepper
1½ cups spinach, chopped
½ lemon, juiced, approx. 2 tablespoons
Garnish Ideas: fresh parsley, red pepper flakes, basil, fresh Italian olives, vegan cheese crumbles

Directions

In a skillet, sauté tomatoes, onion, and garlic in 1 tablespoon olive oil for 2 to 3 minutes, smashing the tomatoes a bit. Add spiralized zucchini, oregano, sea salt, and pepper; cook until al dente, approximately 6 minutes.

Toss in fresh spinach; sauté 1 to 2 minutes; tossing occasionally. Remove from heat; swirl and drizzle in fresh lemon juice and 1 tablespoon olive oil; top with your favorite garnish.

Note:

This recipe was inspired by Chef Steven Loeschner, Integrative Nutrition Health Coach.

Pizza Bowl

Yield 1 serving

Ingredients

3 large garlic cloves, chopped (approx. ¼ cup)

1 cup red onion, chopped

¼ teaspoon sea salt

2 tablespoons olive or avocado oil

½ red bell pepper, sliced (approx. 1 cup)

1 green bell pepper, sliced (approx. 2 cups)

1 cup crimini mushrooms, sliced

2 tablespoon chives, minced, plus more for garnish

2 tablespoons parsley, minced, plus more for garnish

1½–2 tablespoons 25 Star white balsamic vinegar (I recommend the Olive Pantry's)

1½ tablespoons pizza seasoning (I recommend Frontier Co-Op)

2 cups spinach, chopped

2 large dark red heirloom tomatoes, chopped (approx. 1½–2 cups)

¼ teaspoon red pepper flakes

¼ teaspoon oregano (optional)

Garnish Ideas: red pepper flakes, nutritional yeast, hemp seeds, parsley, chives, artichoke hearts, sundried tomatoes

Directions

In a cast-iron skillet sauté garlic, onion, and sea salt in olive oil, stirring occasionally until onions caramelize, approximately 5 minutes. Add bell peppers and mushrooms; sauté an additional 4 minutes until tender. Add chives, parsley, balsamic vinegar, pizza seasoning, spinach, and tomato with juices; stir and cook for approximately another 2 to 3 minutes. Ladle servings into bowls and top with your favorite garnish.

Notes:

Best if tomatoes are chopped in a food processor to reserve the liquid; add chopped tomato with liquid to the sauté pan.

If you are not on the intermittent detox cleanse, you may serve your pizza bowl over steamed brown or wild rice cooked with vegetable broth for added flavor.

Sloppy Jane Butter Lettuce Wrap

Yield 4–6 servings

Ingredients for Sloppy Jane
1 red onion, sliced, chopped
4 garlic cloves, minced
2 tablespoons olive oil
½ teaspoon cumin
½ teaspoon sea salt
1½ cup brown lentils
½ cup orange lentils
1¾ cup carrots, shredded, approx. 3 carrots
4½ cups vegetable broth
3 tablespoons organic vegetarian Worcestershire sauce (I recommend Annie's)
¾ cup organic barbeque sauce (I recommend Annie's), plus extra for building lettuce
    wrap
2 tablespoons maple syrup
1 teaspoon paprika
2 teaspoons smoked paprika
2 tablespoons organic sundried tomato paste
Handful mustard greens, chopped
Dash cayenne

Ingredients for building one wrap
Butter lettuce leaf for wrap
1 teaspoon spicy brown mustard
1 teaspoon barbeque sauce (I recommend Annie's)
¼ avocado, sliced

In a deep skillet sauté onion and garlic in olive oil until caramelized; approximately 5 to 7 minutes, stirring occasionally. Add all other ingredients for Sloppy Jane; bring to a boil, reduce heat to low boil, cover and cook until lentils are very tender, approximately 45 minutes plus or minus (see note below). Remove lid and cook uncovered until thickened.

Drizzle spicy brown mustard and a bit of barbeque sauce onto a butter lettuce leaf, dollop ¼ cup Sloppy Jane mixture, and devour. You can add just about anything you like to your Sloppy Jane: pickles, tomato, green olives. Go wild!

Note:

Cooking unsprouted lentils, cook times may vary. Be sure to add water when appropriate and/or up the cooking time. Cooking sprouted lentils, cook times will be reduced. Organic Accents Sprouted Lentil Trio by truRoots can be purchased at most supermarkets.

by Rachel Feldman

For 7,000 years, people have been fermenting certain foods, such as grapes for fine wine. The foods are "cultured" using microorganisms such as beneficial bacteria, yeasts, or fungi to produce a flavorful taste, preserve the product naturally, and provide a wide range of health benefits. Two commonly known cultured foods are yogurt and sauerkraut.

Fermented, or cultured, foods produce organisms called probiotics, a term that means "for life." These organisms play an important role in balancing the gut's good bacteria, enhancing the immune system, and keeping the intestinal tract in good condition. They help break down nutrients into a more digestible form, increasing the level and effectiveness of the nutrients. This helps suppress the *Helicobacter pylori* (H. pylori) bacteria that can cause gastrointestinal disease.

But that's not all. Probiotics from fermented foods help destroy or prevent the mutation of cancer cells through detoxification, strengthen the immune system, and flush heavy metals. Thus, they help to maintain the colon's proper pH, or acidity level.

Cultured foods also help reduce symptoms of lactose intolerance such as diarrhea and keep other gastrointestinal diseases at bay. They help maintain low cholesterol and a healthy liver and reduce inflammation caused by rheumatoid arthritis and other inflammatory or bowel diseases. They promote weight control, thus reducing the risk of cardiovascular diseases and diabetes. The healthful compounds in these foods have antihypertensive properties that thin the blood, protect the blood vessels, and help improve the pulmonary system.

Nourishing nutrients derived from fermented foods include calcium, protein, B vitamins, manganese, vitamin C, nattokinase, and dietary folates.

Following are recipes for two cultured foods. Here's to your health!

—Rachel Feldman
Health Coach Turned Business Coach
www.rachelafeldman.com

Homemade Coconut Water Kefir

by Rachel Feldman

Yield 1 serving

Ingredients

½ cup water kefir grains
2 to 4 cups fresh young Thai coconut water

Directions

Prep your ingredients. Fill a 4-cup glass jar with wide opening and a tight lid (mason jars work well) with young Thai coconut water and add water kefir grains. Stir with a non-metal spatula as metal will damage the grains. Close the jar, making sure it's airtight, and let it stand for 24 to 48 hours. (The longer it sits, the more bacteria you have cultured.)

Strain the kefir. Open the jar filled with coconut water and kefir grains. Strain the contents through a plastic sieve into a bowl. Refill the glass jars with the cultured coconut water. Make sure the glass jars are airtight. Refrigerate for one to two days and serve chilled.

Variations: To make lemon or lime coconut water kefir, add ¼ cup lemon or lime juice to 1 quart of coconut water kefir. To make cherry coconut water kefir, add ½ cup cherry concentrate to 1 quart of coconut water kefir.

Homemade Must-Have Cultured Vegetables

by Rachel Feldman

Yield 4 serving

Ingredients

Starter culture
1 large head of cabbage, shredded
1 bunch kale, chopped
1 lemon, juiced

2 carrots, shredded
1 clove garlic
¼ cup brine from veggie starter culture
1 large grape leaf, set to the side

Directions

Combine shredded cabbage, kale, lemon juice, carrots, and garlic in a large bowl. Pour prepared brine over the vegetables and squeeze the mixture together for 2 to 5 minutes. Little by little start to add the entire mixture into a large mason jar, along with the liquid; press down firmly with a wooden spoon. The brine will rise to the top as you tightly compact the vegetables toward the bottom of the jar; cover with a large grape leaf and press down firmly.

Allow your vegetables to ferment at room temperature for five days before tasting them—or longer until they achieve the desired sour taste. Transfer to cold storage.

Notes:

Tannin-rich leaves will provide a crispier cultured vegetable and prevent mold during fermentation; these include grape leaf, oak leaf, or kale leaf. Choose one desired leaf to top your vegetables during the process.

Veggie starter culture can be purchased at www.bodyecology.com or www.culturesforhealth.com. Prepare veggie starter culture as per the product's directions to create brine.

Shchi Sauerkraut and Mushroom Soup

Yield 6 servings

Ingredients

4 cups vegetable broth
3 red potatoes, diced
2 bay leaves
1 yellow onion, sliced
2 carrots, shredded
1–2 tablespoons olive oil or coconut oil (for sauté)
Healthy pinch sea salt and pepper
⅛ teaspoon pepper
⅓ cup dried porcini, soaked (or fresh shitake or preferred mushroom)
1½–2 cups sauerkraut (page 170)
Garnish Ideas: vegan sour cream and fresh dill

Directions

In a large saucepan, bring broth, potatoes, and bay leaves to a boil; reduce heat and slow boil for 15 minutes or until potatoes are fork tender. While the potatoes are cooking, sauté onion and carrots in oil for 5 to 7 minutes with a healthy pinch of sea salt and pepper. Wash sauerkraut and drain to remove sour or vinegar taste; set aside. Soak dried porcini in water for 10 minutes; drain.

Five minutes before the potatoes are done, add all ingredients to the soup: sautéed onion and carrot, sauerkraut, and mushrooms. Stir and cook the last 5 minutes and serve with fresh dill and sour cream.

Homemade Sauerkraut

Yield 8 servings

Ingredients
1 head green or purple cabbage, sliced, discard core
1 carrot, shred, ends removed (optional)
1 tablespoons sea salt
1 bay leaf (optional)

Directions
Combine sliced cabbage, carrot, and sea salt into a large bowl; squeeze for 5–10 minutes until it yields liquid. Tightly pack a mason jar with the cabbage, including all the liquid, and bay leaf. Press down firmly and place a small cup weighted with pennies, marbles, or pebbles over the top to keep the cabbage submerged in brine. Cover with cheesecloth and secure with twine or a rubber band. Set on countertop to ferment 4 to 7 (up to 14 days) at room temperature. After approximately a day, remove the small weighted cup. Your kraut should be submerged by now on its own. Recover and check it daily. Small bubbles will form. This is a good sign your fermentation is in progress. The color of your cabbage will change from purple to pink and/or green to more of a yellow.

   Give those lil' pups a taste on day 4, day 5, and so on until you have created the ideal taste, then refrigerate.

French Onion Soup

Yield 4 servings

3 yellow onions, sliced and chopped
1 garlic clove, smashed
3 tablespoons coconut oil
¼ teaspoon sea salt
Healthy pinch black pepper
1 tablespoon coconut vinegar
2 tablespoons Star white balsamic vinegar
2¾ cups vegetable broth
¼ cup coconut aminos
½ teaspoon fresh thyme leaves
Garnish with a bit of sourdough bread slathered in vegan butter, ¼ cup shredded vegan Daiya cheese per soup bowl.

Directions

Using a large cast-iron skillet, sauté onions and garlic in coconut oil, along with sea salt and pepper, for 10 minutes, stirring occasionally. Cover with foil and roast in a preheated oven at 400 degrees for 1 hour. Remove from the oven, remove foil, and place the skillet back on the stovetop; turn heat to medium and drizzle with coconut vinegar; scrape the caramelized onion from the sides and bottom of the saucepan and stir. Now drizzle balsamic vinegar and add vegetable broth, coconut aminos, and fresh thyme; bring to a low boil and cook for 10 minutes.

Ladle a bit of French onion soup into a bowl, top with a small piece of toasted sourdough slathered in vegan butter, sprinkle with Daiya cheese, and broil, if you wish, under a toaster oven or broiler for 3 to 5 minutes to create a sizzling, cheese-melting amazingly delicious French Onion Soup. Add up to ¾ cup additional vegetable broth for a milder flavor.

Lentil Soup

Yield 4 servings

Ingredients

1 cup brown lentils
1 teaspoon cumin
1 teaspoon oregano
1 yellow onion, chopped
2 carrots, chopped
3–4 celery stalks, chopped
2 bay leaves
½ teaspoon sea salt
2 cups low-sodium vegetable broth
2–3 cups water
Garnish with a bit of sourdough bread slathered in vegan butter, fresh parsley, oregano, thyme and/or dill, cayenne pepper, and/or red pepper flakes

Directions

Wash and rinse lentils, remove debris, and add lentils, along with all other ingredients, to a slow cooker. Cook on high for 4 hours or low for 8 hours. Ladle a bit of Lentil Soup into a bowl, top with a small piece of toasted sourdough slathered in vegan butter, and sprinkle with any or all of your favorite garnish.

Be creative and add any of your favorite vegetables to the soup before cooking: tomatoes, zucchini, fresh herbs, or spices.

Mediterranean Northern Bean Soup

Yield 6 servings

Ingredients
1 cup northern white beans, presoaked overnight; drain
3 cups vegetable broth
1½–2 cups water
½ red onion, minced
1 garlic clove, minced
1 tablespoon olive oil
2 red bell peppers, minced
½ teaspoon Mediterranean seasoning (I recommend Spicely Organics)
2 bay leaves
½ teaspoon sea salt
¼ teaspoon chili powder
¼ teaspoon red pepper flakes

Directions
Combine soaked beans, broth, and water in a large saucepan; bring to a boil. Reduce heat to a low boil, cover ajar, and cook for 1 hour and 45 minutes.

While the beans are cooking, sauté onion and garlic in olive oil in a separate skillet for 10 minutes; stirring occasionally until onions caramelize. Add red bell pepper and continue to sauté an additional 5 minutes.

Scrape the sauté into the cooking beans, drop in bay leaves; continue to cook beans 15 to 20 minutes until they are done and add sea salt, chili powder, and red pepper flakes. Remove from heat when beans are soft and enjoy. For a bit thicker and creamier soup, remove ½ cup beans with broth; puree in a blender and add back to the soup and stir.

Red Lentil and Caramelized Onion Soup

Yield 6 servings

Ingredients

1 cup red lentils, sorted and rinsed
4 cups vegetable broth
1 bay leaf
1 small yellow onion, diced
Pinch sea salt
1 tablespoon coconut oil
2 carrots shredded, approx. 1 heaping cup full
Garnish with fresh chopped mint and/or Aleppo red pepper flakes

Directions

Bring lentils and vegetable broth to a boil in a saucepan, add bay leaf, reduce heat, cover, and cook on low boil for approximately 30 to 40 minutes until soft. While the lentils are cooking, prepare the vegetables. Sauté onion with a pinch of sea salt in coconut oil in a small skillet for 10 minutes, stirring occasionally until caramelized. Add carrots to the caramelized onion, stir, and sauté for an additional 3 minutes.

By this time, the lentils should be close to done. Pour sautéed vegetables into the saucepan and stir to combine them with the lentils. Cover and cook until lentils and carrots are cooked through. Ladle a bit of Red Lentil and Caramelized Onion Soup into your bowl and top with your favorite garnish.

Shepherd's Pie

Yield 2 servings

Ingredients for filling
1 cup black lentils
3 cups vegetable broth
1 garlic clove, minced
⅓ cup peas
½ teaspoon Dukka seasoning
½ teaspoon sea salt
1 tablespoon lemon, juiced

Ingredients for potato topping
5 small Yukon potatoes, cubed 1-inch thick
Pinch sea salt
1 tablespoon vegan butter substitute (such as Soy-free Earth Balance Buttery Spread)

Directions for filling
Combine lentils, broth, garlic, peas, Dukka and sea salt in a slow cooker; cook on high for 7 to 8 hours until the beans are tender. Pour into a small 9 by 9-inch casserole dish and add lemon juice; set aside.

Directions for potato topping
Combine potato and sea salt in a large pot of water; boil for 25 minutes. Drain thoroughly and place into a large bowl with butter substitute and salt; whisk with beaters until fluffy and spread over lentils. Bake at 350°F for 15 minutes.

Garam Masala Chickpeas

Yield 2 servings

Ingredients

1 tablespoon olive oil
½ onion, minced
1 garlic clove, minced
Pinch of sea salt
1 can chickpeas, drained and rinsed
3 large heirloom tomatoes
1 ginger sliver, minced
2 teaspoons garam masala
½ teaspoon cumin
¼ teaspoon coriander
½ teaspoon paprika
Pinch turmeric
Dash of cayenne pepper
¼ cup coconut cream (see note, page 148)
Garnish with fresh parsley and/or cilantro

Directions

Use olive oil to sauté onion, garlic, and sea salt in a saucepan over medium heat for 5 minutes. While sautéing, rinse chickpeas under warm water, rolling them around; remove skins and discard. Puree tomatoes in a blender. Combine chickpeas, tomato puree, ginger, and spices in a saucepan and bring to a boil; reduce to simmer, cover and cook for 15 minutes.

Uncover, stir in coconut cream, and simmer an additional 5 minutes. Remove from heat and allow to thicken for a few minutes.

Dollop a scoop of Mashed Cauliflower (page 185) onto your plate and top with Garam Masala Chickpeas and top with your favorite garnish.

Mashed Cauliflower

Yield 2–4 servings

Ingredients

1 head cauliflower, florets removed
2 tablespoons Earth Balance butter substitute
2 teaspoons nutritional yeast
¼ teaspoon sea salt
⅛ cup vegetable broth
Garnish with a bit more vegan butter substitute, sea salt, nutritional yeast and chives, if desired.

Directions

Fill a large saucepan with 6 inches of water and bring to a boil. Place a steamer basket full of cauliflower florets on top, cover, and steam for approximately 15 minutes or until fork tender.

Remove steamer basket; set aside. Pour out the boiling water. Pour steamed florets into the empty saucepan and add all other ingredients. Use an immersion hand blender and blend until your desired consistency.

This is by far the best cauliflower mash I've ever had. The broth gives it a rich flavor unlike mashes that contain milk.

Dessert Bar

Sweet Tart Cheesecake

Yield 8 servings

1 cup frozen cranberries, thawed
2 lemons juiced, approx. ¾ cup juice
2 tablespoons maple syrup
Dash cinnamon

Ingredients for coconut cream
2 cans coconut cream (see note, page 148)
¼ cup maple syrup
Pinch sea salt
2 teaspoons alcohol-free vanilla extract
3 tablespoons lemon, juiced

Ingredients for crust
10 dates, pitted, chopped, soaked 20 minutes, drained
1½ cup walnuts, soaked 4 hours, drained
¾ cup macaroon coconut flakes

Directions
Combine all ingredients for cranberry sauce in a high-speed blender; blend until creamy; set aside. Makes approximately 12 ounces.

Combine all ingredients for coconut cream in a bowl and whip vigorously with a electric mixer until peaks rise; slowly introduce all but 4 to 6 ounces of cranberry sauce; whip well. Pour remaining cranberry sauce in a mason jar and refrigerate for a drizzling garnish.

Combine all ingredients for crust in a food processor; process on high until mealy, approximately 1 minute. You may need to use a spatula to scrape down the edges during processing.

Line the bottom of a small 6-inch springform cake pan with parchment paper; fill with crust and press firmly. Slowly pour your whipped Sweet Tart Cheesecake filling over the top and freeze for 4 hours. Before slicing, thaw on the countertop for 15 to 20 minutes; drizzle a bit of cranberry sauce over your slice and sprinkle with macaroon coconut flakes and enjoy. Keep remainder frozen until devoured.

Coconut Whipped Cream and Strawberries

Yield 1–2 servings

Ingredients

1 cup coconut cream (see note on page 148)
½ teaspoon vanilla bean powder or 1 teaspoon alcohol-free vanilla extract
2 tablespoons agave or maple syrup
Handful strawberries

Directions

Extremely addicting sweet coconut whipped cream: Blend coconut cream, vanilla, and agave in a large mixing bowl with an electric mixer until there are light and fluffy peaks of cream. Using a frosting pipe bag, swirl layers of cream and chopped strawberries into a glass and enjoy. Store remaining coconut whipped cream in the refrigerator until it's time for your next dessert.

Fried Apple and Walnut Crisp

Yield 1 serving

Ingredients

1 apple, your choice, cored, thinly sliced
1 tablespoon unrefined coconut oil
¼ cup walnuts, premeasured then roughly chopped
¼ teaspoon Chinese 5-spice powder
Garnish Ideas: drizzle of honey or maple syrup and a dash of cinnamon

Directions

Preheat cast-iron skillet with coconut oil, toss in apple and walnuts; sauté for 2 minutes. Add Chinese 5-spice powder and sauté for an additional 3 minutes; add to a small plate and drizzle with honey or maple syrup and a dash of cinnamon. Spice it up a bit and add a dash of cayenne. I love cayenne in just about everything!

Raw Vegan Carrot Cake

Yield 4–6 servings

Ingredients for cake
2 cups carrots, grated, approx. 3 carrots
12 dates, pitted, diced, soaked for 20 min, drain
1 cup cashews or pecans, soaked for at least 2 hours, drain
1 cup dried macaroon coconut flakes
1 teaspoon cinnamon
⅛ teaspoon allspice
½ cup dried cranberries or raisins

Ingredients for frosting
1 cup coconut cream (see note on page 148)
2 tablespoons maple syrup
Pinch sea salt
1 teaspoon alcohol-free vanilla extract
1½ tablespoons lemon, juiced

Directions
Combine all ingredients for cake in a food processor and process on high until mealy; approximately 1 minute. Do not overprocess. You may need to stop the food processor intermittently to scrape down the sides. Line a small 4-or 6-inch springform cake pan with coconut oil or parchment paper; fill with carrot cake batter and press firmly.

Combine all frosting ingredients in a bowl and whip with a electric mixer until peaks develop. Layer frosting over carrot cake, refrigerate for a few hours, and enjoy. You may opt to layer your carrot cake by spreading half of the carrot cake batter, then a bit of frosting, another layer of cake batter, then another layer of frosting.

Cantaloupe Crush Ice Pops and Soft Serve

Yield 8 servings

Ingredients

1 sweet ripe cantaloupe, peeled and diced; freeze solid
2 tablespoons water
Ice pop trays (optional)

Directions

Combine frozen cantaloupe chunks and water in a high-speed blender and blend until creamy; pour into glass and enjoy as a cantaloupe crush soft serve or into ice pop trays; freeze solid for a refreshing and healthy summer treat.

Special Bonus Recipes

Overnight Oats

Yield 1 serving

Ingredients
½ cup heaping rolled oats
1 teaspoon quinoa (optional)
1 teaspoon chia seeds
¾ cup almond, coconut, or other preferred mylk
½ banana, sliced
1 tablespoon shaved 80 percent organic dark chocolate or macaroon coconut flakes

Directions
Combine oats, quinoa, chia seeds, and mylk in a serving glass or mason jar; give it a little whirl. Drop in banana and top with shaved chocolate or macaroon coconut flakes; refrigerate overnight. Grab and go the next morning.

Note:
Add a teaspoon of maple syrup for a sweet treat.

Tomato Basil Gazpacho

Yield 2 servings

Ingredients
3 vine-ripened tomatoes, divided
2 inches English cucumber, diced
1 garlic, minced
½ red bell pepper, diced
½ green bell pepper, diced
1 tablespoon fresh basil, minced
1 tablespoon olive oil
2 tablespoons lemon, juiced
½ teaspoon sea salt
Dash pepper

Directions

Core 2 tomatoes and slice in half. Place the tomato seed side against a handheld grater, and shred tomato over a bowl by sliding it back and forth until only the skin remains; discard tomato skins. Pour tomato liquid into a high-speed blender and blend for 45 seconds until creamy; set aside.

Core and dice 1 tomato; pour into a large bowl and add all remaining ingredients; top with creamy tomato from the blender and stir. Divide and ladle into two small serving glasses and chill in the refrigerator for at least an hour.

Note:

You can find this recipe and more like it in *The Green Aisle's Healthy Indulgence.*

Cast-Iron Potato Pie

Yield 4 servings

Ingredients
6 red potatoes
1 tablespoon coconut oil
1 teaspoon sea salt
3 dash cayenne
½ teaspoon paprika
Cracked pepper

Directions
Rough chop potatoes to fit inside a food processor; pulse until the size of rice grains. Place in a fine mesh strainer and rinse until water runs clear to remove excess starch.

Grease a cast-iron skillet with coconut oil; layer potato, top with seasonings and bake at 450°F for 30 minutes, broil for 5 minutes to give the top a nice crunch, and serve.

Note:
Be creative with this recipe and try adding your favorite chopped greens, herbs, or veggies to the mix: mustard greens, spinach, kale, collards, cilantro, oregano, bell peppers, olives, stewed tomatoes, onion, garlic. Variations are endless. Go wild!

Jade Pearl Rice Ramen

Yield 2 servings

Ingredients

1 Jade Pearl Rice Ramen patty by Lotus Foods
1 green bell pepper, minced
1 cup mustard greens, chopped
1 tablespoon parsley, minced
1 carrot, shredded
2 cups vegetable broth
2 tablespoons Sweet Ginger Chili by the Ginger People
2 tablespoons tamari
Dash cayenne
½ teaspoon sea salt

Directions

Combine all ingredients, except rice ramen patty, into a saucepan; bring to boil, reduce to low boil for 6 minutes. Add rice ramen patty. When the noodles start to unfold, separate them with a fork and continue to cook on a low boil for 3 to 4 minutes; serve.

Quinoa Tabbouli Salad

Yield 6 servings

Ingredients
¼ cup quinoa
1 medium-sized onion, minced
5 cups parsley, minced
¼ cup mint, minced
3 large tomatoes, diced
½ green pepper (optional)
1 small Persian cucumber
½ cup lemon, juiced
¼ cup olive oil
Pinch sea salt, pepper, and cinnamon

Directions
Wash quinoa and drain well. Cook as directed on the package; set aside. In a large bowl, combine and mix onions with sea salt, pepper, and cinnamon until onion turns brownish. Add quinoa, parsley, mint, and tomatoes; toss. Drizzle lemon juice and olive oil and combine.

Note:
This recipe was inspired by Rania Chami, Holistic Health and Wellness Coach.

10-Minute Veggie Stir-Fry

Yield 1–2 servings

Ingredients
1 tablespoon peanut oil
½ cup onion, sliced
1 small zucchini, cut into matchstick strips
1 red bell pepper, cut into matchstick strips
1 orange bell pepper, cut into matchstick strips
Handful fresh string beans
1 jalapeño, sliced
1 tablespoon tamari
1 tablespoon toasted sesame oil
Healthy pinch sea salt
Garnish with chopped cilantro or sesame seeds (optional)

Directions
Sauté onion in peanut oil for 2 minutes; add zucchini, bell pepper, string beans, and jalapeño, sprinkle a pinch of sea salt. Continue to sauté for 5 minutes, tossing occasionally. Reduce heat, add tamari and toasted sesame oil; stir and remove from heat. Serve with steamed rice.

Note:
Save time, money, and hot fingers by buying jalapeños in bulk and freezing them. When you're ready, just rinse one under water, pat dry, and slice while cold.

Raw Vegan Fudge

Yield 25 servings

Ingredients
¼ cup cocoa powder
¾ cup cacao powder*
1 cup maple syrup
½ cup natural peanut butter**
2 teaspoons vanilla extract
¾ teaspoon sea salt
Small handful pistachios, sliced (optional)***
¾ cup cacao butter, melted

Directions
Pour all ingredients into a high-speed blender, pouring in the melted cacao butter last. Blend on high until creamy. Pour into a small casserole dish lined with parchment paper and refrigerate for 15 minutes. Remove from the fridge and pop out the fudge by turning the dish upside down. Slice into 1-inch chunks and enjoy.

Note:
*Raw cacao butter can be purchased on Amazon or found in your local health food market.

**Change your flavor by changing out the butters and/or extracts: cashew butter, hazelnut butter, etc, or almond extract, peppermint, etc.

***You can opt to use any nuts you prefer or no nuts at all if you like your fudge creamy and smooth.

Coconut Cream Cheese Fruit Rice Cake

Cream cheese yields 8 servings (2 tablespoons each)

Ingredients
½ cup coconut cream (see note on page 148)
½ cup vegan cream cheese by Daiya Foods
1 teaspoon alcohol-free vanilla extract
2 tablespoons maple syrup
1 Organic Honey Nut Rice Cake per serving

Directions

Extremely addicting sweet coconut cream cheese. Blend coconut cream, Daiya Foods, vanilla extract, and maple in a large mixing bowl with an electric mixer until there are light and fluffy peaks of cream. If your cream is not peaking and firm, freeze the entire bowl for 10 minutes or so; mix again with electric mixer. Dollop 2 tablespoons coconut cream cheese per 1 rice cake; top with your favorite fruits and enjoy. Store remaining coconut cream cheese in the refrigerator until it's time for your next dessert.

Note:

Garnish with all your favorite fruits: strawberries, nectarines, blueberries, raspberries, cherries—use as many will fit on your rice cake.

Orange Blueberry Infusion

Yield 2 servings, 16 ounces

Ingredients
16 ounces mineral water or spring water
1 orange, sliced
½ cup blueberries
9 mint leaves

Directions
Combine all ingredients in a large mason jar, cover and refrigerate overnight to infuse flavors.

Rosemary and Lemon Infusion

Yield 2 servings, 16 ounces

Ingredients
16 ounces water
1 lemon wedge + 2 lemon slices
1 sprig fresh rosemary
Pinch Himalayan pink salt (optional)

Directions
Squeeze a little bit of lemon into the bottom of your mason jar, add pink salt and drop in the lemon, add rosemary, and pour water over the top. Cover and refrigerate overnight to infuse flavors.

Peppermint Mocha Scrub

FUN DIY RECIPES

It's wise to pay attention to what you put on your body, as well as in it. Many commercial products for self-care contain toxic ingredients that can be detrimental to your health. Have a go at the following recipes. Treat yourself to safe, fun self-care products that support the vibrant health you're developing, along with your new eating habits. Although these creations are intended for external use, their names sound yummy enough to eat. Enjoy using them for skin, lip, and tooth care!

Peppermint Mocha Scrub

Yield 1 cup

Ingredients

¼ cup unrefined coconut oil, melted
1 cup organic unbleached pure cane
   sugar

3 tablespoons ground organic coffee
   beans
10 drops essential peppermint oil

Directions

Mix all ingredients in a 4-ounce mason jar, cover, and seal. Wet a soft baby cloth, scoop a tablespoon of scrub onto the cloth and rub onto any dry or rough areas on the body in a circular motion, rinse, and pat dry. Especially refreshing to awaken to coffee and peppermint in the mornings!

Dreamsicle Lip Balm

Yields 2 lip balm tubes

Ingredients

1 tablespoon cocoa butter, melted
1 tablespoon shea butter
1 teaspoon unrefined coconut oil

15 drops essential wild orange oil
2 empty lip balm tubes

Directions

Place cocoa butter in a very small saucepan and simmer on the lowest temperature until completely melted. While the cocoa butter is melting, combine shea butter, coconut oil, and essential oil into a small mixing bowl; pour melted cocoa butter over the top and whisk thoroughly. By using a turkey baster or syringe, you can fill your lip balm tubes. Refrigerate for a few hours until solid, then secure the cap. Moisturize lips any time of the day; apply softly. Keep lip balm from extreme temperatures (over 93–101°F) as it will start to melt.

Peppermint Fluoride-Free Toothpaste

Ingredients

1 tablespoon unrefined organic coconut oil
1 tablespoon baking soda
1–3 drop of spearmint, peppermint,
   or other preferred essential oil (optional)
Small container with resealable lid

Directions

Whisk coconut oil, baking soda, and essential oil in a small container; cover and store in cupboard. No need to refrigerate. The baking soda whitens your teeth, while the coconut oil kills unfriendly bacteria.

Use a soft-bristle brush and clean your toothbrush as needed with a hydrogen peroxide dip, or dip it in a mixture consisting of ½ cup water, 2 tablespoons vinegar, and 2 teaspoons baking soda to keep it free of germs; rinse well.

Notes:

Some brands of baking soda are polluted with benzene and most brands contain aluminum even if it does not mention this in the ingredients. Aluminum is linked to Alzheimer's disease and cancer. Make sure your baking soda says specifically "aluminum free."

Fluoride is contained in many commercial toothpastes. Fluoride causes us to absorb extra aluminum. It destroys enzymes that deliver phosphate to calcium at the tooth surface needed for strong teeth and is biological poison.

These pastes also may contain sodium lauryl sulfate (SLS), which the American College of

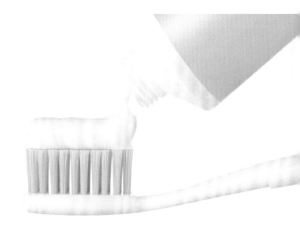

Toxicity states is corrosive and harmful to skin tissue. It is used in cleaning products and engine degreasers. You get the picture.

Viscous, sticky glycerin is also added, coating the teeth. Ever wonder why there is a warning label on those commercial brand toothpastes? Now you know!

Eco-friendly toothbrushes? Have you ever thought of the little things we take for granted? Or the big things, for that matter, like our Planet Earth? If millions of people change out their regular toothbrushes as recommended every few months, where does that leave our precious planet? Full of nonbiodegradable plastics—that's where!

You can get a natural bamboo toothbrush that's eco-friendly. Give these little bamboo pups a try!

F.A.Q.

Frequently Asked Questions from happy clients:

Q: I'm going to a big block party and need to bring a cold salad. I know I should probably stick to juice, but I'm wondering if there's a cold salad that would be okay for me to have.
A: Sticking to the schedule will yield better results, but as we know, bio-individuality comes into play (for some, it is extremely difficult to detox). You can whip up my Tomato Basil Gazpacho or Cabbage Lime Fresca.

Q: Does doing this detox require you to stay home and close to the bathroom?
A: No. Maybe number "1" with all the liquid; but no worries about number "2" or "3."

Q: I don't own a juicing machine but have a Ninja. Is that something I can use, or do I need to go buy a juicer?
A: You can use a blender or Ninja to blend the vegetables. Just add a bit of water and strain the mixture either through cheesecloth or a nut mylk bag.

Q: Is there a grocery list for this detox?
A: The recipes are here as a guide. Since we are all bio-individuals, what one person likes may not be what another person likes. There are plenty of delicious recipes to choose from. Once you've pick what appeals to you from your scheduled guide, you can purchase the ingredients on the list.

About the Author

Integrative nutrition health coach and author **Michelle Savage** helps those suffering from gut-related and/or weight issues to gain vibrant health and empower them to live an energized and happy life. Her tasty recipes blend organic juices, smoothies, and whole-plant-based meals for eliminating body toxins, boosting energy, and creating vibrant health. She also offers personalized one-on-one health coaching to help clients confidently prepare healthy meals and revitalize their lifestyle.

Books

Everyone likes to eat, and Michelle believes that eating healthy can be fun and feel good. Besides *The Green Aisle's Healthy Juicing,* she's authored two other game-changing books on healthy, rewarding eating and lifestyle transformation: *The Green Aisle's Healthy Smoothies and Slushies* and *The Green Aisle's Healthy Indulgence* (Skyhorse Publishing). Illustrated with colorful, mouthwatering photographs, these books offer some of the best satisfying and appealing healthy recipes on the market. You'll find recipes inspired by locations and cuisines around the world: Thai Shrimp Soup, Russian Borscht, Israeli Shakshouka, Armenian Dolma, Greek Pizza, plus Coconut Cream Pie Smoothies, Strawberry Shortcake Smoothies, and much, much more!

Education and Coaching

Besides her inspired creativity with food, Michelle is equipped with extensive, cutting-edge knowledge in holistic health practices and disease prevention. She's a graduate of the Institute for Integrative Nutrition, and a certified integrative nutrition health coach who has received specialized training in gut health. Her approach focuses on building a sustainable and positive relationship with healthy eating and making changes that produce real and lasting results. She helps clients go beyond dieting and calorie counting and develop a deeper understanding of intuitive eating.

Michelle believes in bio-individuality, encouraging lifestyle shifts that work best for each of her clients, thus improving their energy, balance, health, and happiness. Reversing GI-related symptoms and achieving lasting weight loss are by-products as clients experience joy and confidence with their newfound healthy way of life.

Michelle walks her talk. She learned from experience what creative, healthy eating can do when she reclaimed control of her own health and life. Her personal journey ignited a passion for helping others to build confidence and get lasting health results—all while enjoying a creative approach to eating nutritious, delicious food.

Thanks to Michelle's personalized coaching program in integrative nutrition, now you, too, can learn how to reshape your relationship with food and revitalize your body and life. If you'd like to book an initial consultation, please visit: www.GreenAisleWellness.com or http://www.greenaislewellness.com/my-approach/.

Michelle Savage
Green Aisle Health & Wellness
668 Industrial Park
Suite 4172
Manteca, California 95337
www.GreenAisleWellness.com

Influential Experts

The following top health and wellness experts had a significant influence on Michelle's approach to health and nutrition. She studied their work through the Institute for Integrative Nutrition headquartered in New York City. (www.integrativenutrition.com).

- Joshua Rosenthal, MScEd, Founder and Director of the Institute for Integrative Nutrition
- Deepak Chopra, MD, World Leader in Mind-Body Medicine, Director of Education at The Chopra Center, bestselling author
- David Katz, MD, MPH, authority on preventive medicine and weight management, Director of the Yale Prevention Research Center
- Walter Willett, MD, DrPH, Chair of the Department of Nutrition, Harvard's School of Public Health, and bestselling author
- Andrew Weil, MD, expert on integrative medicine and mind-body interactions, bestselling author
- Gabrielle Bernstein, motivational speaker, life coach, bestselling author
- Susan Blum, MD, MPH, Functional Medicine Doctor, Founder of Blum Center for Health
- Mark Hyman, MD, Founder and Medical Director of The UltraWellness Center, bestselling author
- Geneen Roth, pioneer of emotional eating and empowerment, bestselling author
- David Wolfe, recognized expert on superfoods and raw nutrition and bestselling author
- Marion Nestle, PhD, MPH, Paulette Goddard Professor of Nutrition, Food Studies and Public Health at New York University
- Mark Bittman, *New York Times* columnist, bestselling author

Testimonials

Meet more happy clients!

Tammy Dean Nicholl, Age 52, Discovery Bay, CA

Beauty and Style Photographer—tdnphotography.com

I want to take this opportunity to thank Michelle of Green Aisle Wellness for all of her compassion and passion to heal and change peoples' lives. Although I haven't been officially diagnosed, my daughter was, took all of the necessary testing, and it was determined that she had Hashimoto's thyroiditis. It is autoimmune and also hereditary. Since I had the same exact symptoms as her, I made an appointment immediately with my doctor, which I really didn't feel I needed to wait for a doctor to instruct me on what to do next. I met Michelle around the same time, and she was determined to get me started on the necessary nutrition and diet plan along with supplements. Started me off with curcumin.

I never thought I had inflammation as bad as I actually had. Until about four days into taking curcumin every morning, I noticed that ALL of my bloat was gone, which I thought it was weight gain all of these years! After a week or two of grievance over what I couldn't eat anymore, I started eating what I COULD eat from my fridge and pantry filled with horrible things. And since I was so busy, I didn't have any time to shop for the things that will make me feel better. I would either choose NOT to eat or eat something bad, until I knew WHAT to shop for. I was struggling!

Michelle heard me, but she didn't want to overwhelm me and gave me a few recipes to start off with! Day by day I was gaining momentum and feeling so much energy like I was in my 30s. I will never be able to thank Michelle enough. She went above and beyond to guide me in this direction! I have a long way to go, but feel blessed to know that I have Green Aisle Wellness to guide me along the way! Thank you, Michelle!

Tammy and Michelle. Photo credit: Tammy Dean Nicholl, Beauty and Style Photographer

Lynette Smith, Age 65, Manteca, CA

Starting Weight 208 ~ Ending Weight 188

My top two goals upon starting the 6-month program were getting healthy and losing weight. Michelle helped me achieve these goals by teaching me about eating clean, providing recipes, and checking on my progress. The biggest tangible change? I have lost 20 pounds in 10 weeks! The most significant overall change I have noticed has been my feeling of well-being and continue to see and feel the positive results.

Michelle is informative, helpful, eager to help, and I would recommend my health coach to anyone ready to embark on a journey to healthy eating and the feeling of being in control.

My top three goals upon starting the 6-month program were to learn how to make healthier choices with the food I was eating. Michelle was able to show me what different ingredients are that are both good and bad, and also how to make healthier decisions for each meal.

The biggest change I've noticed since beginning the program has been eating healthier options and not feeling so full afterward because what I ate was too heavy or I ate too much.

I would describe my coach as amazing! Very patient and understanding. Also follows up to our meetings well with what we talked about. I would recommend Michelle to anyone that is looking to make a lifestyle change.

I started working with Michelle Savage for many reasons. First, after my divorce, my weight was increasing, causing me to grow weary of my health and appearance. You see, my ex-wife did all the cooking and I had not prepared a complete meal in many years. Not knowing what to do, I either ate out or cooked simple, but not necessarily nutritional meals.

Second, when I decided to make lifestyle changes, I tried to learn about different methods to lose weight and eat healthy. I was quickly overwhelmed and confused from reading conflicting articles and reports on these subjects.

Third, a close friend of mine participated in a medically supervised weight-loss program but still developed health issues. That really worried me.

Starting Weight 201

Then I found author and health and wellness coach Michelle Savage. She met with me for a face-to-face consult and evaluation. After speaking with her, I decided she had the best tools and knowledge to help me become healthy again. It was a great move for me.

After completing 2–3 sessions, I began to feel better and see results. By then, I had stopped eating fast food and consciously reduced my sugar and carb intake. I also started making meals with fresh ingredients. I experienced many unexpected breakthroughs.

Michelle taught me that losing weight is directly related to making healthy choices and not necessarily counting calories. She showed me how to spot and eliminate unhealthy ingredients from my meals. Using her cookbooks and recipes as a founda-

Ending Weight 172

tion, it was easy to make quick and tasty meals. I was pleasantly surprised that my old clothes were beginning to feel loose, and I no longer groaned when I looked in the mirror.

Michelle developed a custom program for my needs to increase my basic food knowledge, develop healthy recipes, and beginner exercise programs. She helped me start collecting healthy recipes and cookbooks. She took me on tours of health food stores and supermarkets for real-life shopping and study. Michelle is always available to answer questions and frequently reached out to gauge and monitor my progress and challenges.

Although my journey is not finished yet, as of today, I have lost nearly 30 pounds and am happily replacing large parts of my wardrobe. I have more energy, feel great, and with Michelle's help have added physical activities to my daily routine. Her cookbooks have a variety of easy and healthy alternative recipes.

I never would have been able to achieve any of this without Michelle's expertise and support. I am certain that I will be able to continue this path for years to come. This is such a great program, I referred my friends to her as well. Thank you, Michelle!

My top three goals upon starting my health coaching program were that I wanted to lose weight, lower my blood sugar, and feel better and I have. My coach was able to help me work toward these goals by giving me inspiration, for one, and for showing me recipes and showing me how to control my diet. The biggest tangible change I have noticed since beginning the program has been more energy! I have lost weight and I feel better.

I would recommend my coach to anyone that would ask me and somebody that would reach out. I really would.

Author's Note: I'm so proud of you, Curtis! In just a few months you've made so many successful accomplishments!

Starting Weight 386 ~
Ending Weight 354

At 386 pounds, nearing stage 4 kidney disease, diagnosed with diabetes, Curtis decided his life was literally dependent upon making a change. Our sessions were sometimes tearful, emotional, but in the end, tears of joy flowed from my eyes and goosebumps appeared as we shared his progress! It's been an amazing journey, and he's only just begun.

Before meeting with me, Curtis has had blood sugar spikes ranging from 260 to 300, was taking insulin 3 times a day, suffered fatigue, and had a poor diet. In just a few short months, you can see his immense smile, vibrant skin, and joy shine through. The day of our last session, his blood sugar was 89 upon waking. He hasn't had the need for insulin injections, lost 22+ pounds, is moving toward great success, and, most of all, he is DOING THE WORK!

Curtis, I want to thank you for taking the time to share your journey and be a true inspiration for others!

Contributors

Rania Chami, Certified Holistic Health and Wellness Coach

Rania decided to become a health coach to fulfill her passion of working with busy moms and families to improve their health and family life. She offers corporate coaching, as well as individual and groups. Contact Rania at healthcoachraina@ gmail.com.
Contributions: Mamma's Hummus, Quinoa Tabbouli Salad

John De La Mora, Insurance Professional.

When John grew tired of his expanding waistline and low energy, he made some big changes that included healthy eating, exercise, and a balanced lifestyle. He's happy and living the good life!
Contributions: Creative and inspiring recipe names and authentic constructive critic taste tester

Bebe Savage, Certified Holistic Health Coach

Contributions: Grass Roots, Brain Teaser

Melissa Kubek, Owner of Organic Cold-pressed Juice & Plant-Based Eats

Contribution: The Juicer Lowdown

Rachel Feldman, Health Coach Turned Business Coach

After struggling with chronic health issues, Rachel found solutions and built a succcessful health coaching business. She then expanded her mission to help new coaches achieve their own thriving businesses and created the Health Coach Done For You Programs at www.yourhealthcoachbiz.com. Through her programs, teaching, and speaking on podcasts and summits, she helps health coaches turn a profit, book more clients, and sell programs of their own. https://yourhealthcoachbiz.com/

Graduate of the Institute for Integrative Nutrition in New York City, Wild Rose Natural College of Healing, the International School of Detoxification, and Natalia Rose Advanced Detox Certification Training.
Contribution: The Benefits of Fermented, or Cultured, Foods

Harley Harris, Creative Home Cook

Contribution: Citrus Sunshine Sexy Smoothie

Steven Loeschner, Integrative Nutrition Health Coach, Chef

Contribution: Italian Zoodles

Resources

The following sources were influential in the writing and researching of this book.

Websites

Albahrani, Ali A., and Ronda F. Greaves. "Fat-Soluble Vitamins: Clinical Indications and Current Challenges for Chromatographic Measurement." *The Clinical Biochemist Reviews*. Posted: February 2016. https://www.ncbi.nlm.nih.gov/pmc/articles/PMC4810759/

"Cherries." *Life Extension Magazine*. Posted: December 2017. http://www.lifeextension.com/Magazine/2007/12/sf_cherries/Page-01

"Eco-Friendly Natural Bamboo Toothbrushes." Amazon.com. http://amzn.to/2nYKh7o

Fluoride Action Committee. "Video: 10 Facts About Fluoride." Posted: April 8, 2013. https://www.youtube.com/watch?v=GX0s-4AyWfI

Hever, Julieanna. "Plant-Based Diets: A Physician's Guide." *The Permanente Journal*. Posted: July 2016. https://www.ncbi.nlm.nih.gov/pmc/articles/PMC4991921/

"Insulin-like Growth Factor 1 (IGF-1)." WhiteLies.org.uk. https://www.whitelies.org.uk/health-nutrition/insulin-growth-factor-1-igf-1

Leech, Joe. "11 Proven Health Benefits of Garlic." Healthline.com. Posted: January 19, 2017. https://www.healthline.com/nutrition/11-proven-health-benefits-of-garlic#section5

"Magnesium in the Diet: The Bad News About Magnesium Food Sources." Ancient-Minerals.com. http://www.ancient-minerals.com/transdermal-magnesium/dietary/

"Meat-Based Diet Linked to Fatty Liver Disease." *The Economic Times*. Posted: April 23, 2017. https://economictimes.indiatimes.com/news/science/meat-based-diet-linked-to-fatty-liver-disease/articleshow/58324095.cms

Mercola, Joseph. "Short Film Reveals the Lunacy of Water Fluoridation." Mercola.com. Posted: June 17, 2017. https://articles.mercola.com/sites/articles/archive/2017/06/17/our-daily-dose-fluoride-documentary.aspx

Pendick, Daniel. "5 Steps for Preventing Kidney Stones." Harvard Medical School. Posted: October 4, 2013. https://www.health.harvard.edu/blog/5-steps-for-preventing-kidney-stones-201310046721

Stein, Natalie. "Can Vitamins Increase Blood Oxygen Level? (Iron Absorption)." Livestrong.com. Posted: August 14, 2017. https://www.livestrong.com/article/492282-vitamins-to-increase-blood-oxygen-level/

Books

Blum, Susan. *The Immune System Recovery Plan*. New York: Scribner, 2013.

Ellison, Shane. *Over the Counter Natural Cures*. New York: Sourcebooks, 2014.

Fowlkes, K. K., and Chuck John. *Wheatgrass, Sprouts, Microgreens, and the Living Food Diet*. Springville, Utah: Living Whole Foods, Inc, 2010.

Gates, Donna, and Linda Schatz. *The Body Ecology Diet: Recovering Your Health and Rebuilding Your Immunity*. Carlsbad, California: Hay House, 2011.

Rosenthal, Joshua. *Integrative Nutrition: Feed Your Hunger for Health and Happiness*. New York: Integrative Nutrition, 2014.

Sandovol, David. *The Green Foods Bible*. Santa Fe, New Mexico: Panacea Publishing, Incorporated, 2015.

Savage, Michelle. *The Green Aisle's Healthy Smoothies & Slushies*. New York: Skyhorse Publishing, 2015.

Savage, Michelle. *The Green Aisle's Healthy Indulgence*. New York, Skyhorse Publishing: 2017.

Somers, Suzanne. *Breakthrough: Eight Steps to Wellness*. New York: Crown Publishing, 2009.

Watson, Brenda. *The Detox Strategy*. New York: Simon & Schuster, 2008.

Index

Conversion Tables

METRIC AND IMPERIAL CONVERSIONS
(These conversions are rounded for convenience)

Ingredient	Cups/Tablespoons/Teaspoons	Ounces	Grams/Milliliters
Protein powder	1 tablespoon	0.3 ounces	8 grams
Coconut flour	1 cup/1 tablespoon	4.5 ounces/ 0.3 ounce	125 grams/8 grams
Fruit, dried	1 cup	4 ounces	120 grams
Fruits or veggies, chopped	1 cup	5 to 7 ounces	145 to 200 grams
Fruits or veggies, puréed	1 cup	8.5 ounces	245 grams
Honey, maple syrup, or agave	1 tablespoon	.75 ounce	20 grams
Liquids: nut milks or water	1 cup	8 fluid ounces	240 milliliters
Gluten-free rolled oats	1 cup	5.5 ounces	150 grams
Salt	1 teaspoon	0.2 ounce	6 grams
Spices: cinnamon, cloves, ginger, or nutmeg (ground)	1 teaspoon	0.2 ounce	5 milliliters
Nut butters	1 cup/1 tablespoon	7 ounces/ 0.5 ounce	200 grams/ 12.5 grams
Vanilla extract	1 teaspoon	0.2 ounce	4 grams